Promoting International Energy Security

Volume 4, The Gulf of Guinea

Stuart E. Johnson, Caroline Baxter,
James T. Bartis, Duncan Long

Prepared for the United States Air Force

RAND PROJECT AIR FORCE

The research described in this report was sponsored by the United States Air Force under Contract FA7014-06-C-0001. Further information may be obtained from the Strategic Planning Division, Directorate of Plans, Hq USAF.

Library of Congress Control Number: 2012948760

ISBN: 978-0-8330-6844-6

The RAND Corporation is a nonprofit institution that helps improve policy and decisionmaking through research and analysis. RAND's publications do not necessarily reflect the opinions of its research clients and sponsors.

RAND® is a registered trademark.

Published 2012 by the RAND Corporation
1776 Main Street, P.O. Box 2138, Santa Monica, CA 90407-2138
1200 South Hayes Street, Arlington, VA 22202-5050
4570 Fifth Avenue, Suite 600, Pittsburgh, PA 15213-2665
RAND URL: http://www.rand.org/
To order RAND documents or to obtain additional information, contact
Distribution Services: Telephone: (310) 451-7002;
Fax: (310) 451-6915; Email: order@rand.org

Preface

The dramatic rise in oil prices in 2008 increased attention on the sources of imported oil, the workings of the world oil market, and the potential problems of meeting future demand for liquid fuels. Energy security concerns typically focus on the Middle East, mainly because that is where surplus oil production capacity is concentrated. But a large amount of the world's oil and natural gas production occurs in countries outside of that area. Political instability, governance shortfalls, conflict, and the potential for further conflict both in and outside the Middle East threaten the reliability of supplies of oil and natural gas.

This is particularly the case in the Gulf of Guinea. In this area, the largest and most important exporter is Nigeria. But a combination of conflict, crime, poor governance, and corruption in Nigeria has suppressed investment in new production and caused the existing production infrastructure to operate at levels well below its designed capacity. Meanwhile, new finds of oil and natural gas have been reported, not only in Nigeria, but also in the territorial waters of Ghana, whose political stability and governance conditions are higher.

In this technical report to the U.S. Air Force, we examine the current security situation in the Gulf of Guinea as relevant to petroleum and natural gas production. Here we find that there are opportunities for the Air Force to build local capabilities to protect the growing off-shore petroleum and natural gas infrastructures. We also discuss the sensitivities that need to be considered in building military capabilities in this region.

This report is the fourth in a four-volume series examining U.S. Air Force roles in promoting international energy security. The research was sponsored by the Office of Operational Planning, Policy and Strategy, Deputy Chief of Staff for Operations, Plans, and Requirements, Headquarters United States Air Force (HQ USAF/A5X), and was undertaken within the Strategy and Doctrine Program of RAND Project AIR FORCE as part of a fiscal year 2010 study "Air Force Roles in Promoting International Energy Security."

The other three volumes in this series are:

- James T. Bartis, *Promoting International Energy Security*, Vol. 1: *Understanding Potential Air Force Roles*, Santa Monica, Calif.: RAND Corporation, TR-1144/1-AF, 2012.
- Andrew S. Weiss, F. Stephen Larrabee, James T. Bartis, and Camille A. Sawak, *Promoting International Energy Security*, Vol. 2: *Turkey and the Caspian*, Santa Monica, Calif.: RAND Corporation, TR-1144/2-AF, 2012.
- Ryan Henry, Christine Osowski, Peter Chalk, and James T. Bartis, *Promoting International Energy Security*, Vol. 3: *Sea-Lanes to Asia*, Santa Monica, Calif.: RAND Corporation, TR-1144/3-AF, 2012.

Readers interested in the topic of energy security may also find the following RAND reports to be of interest.

- James T. Bartis and Lawrence Van Bibber, *Alternative Fuels for Military Applications*, Santa Monica, Calif.: RAND Corporation, MG-969-OSD, 2011.
- Keith Crane, Andreas Goldthau, Michael Toman, Thomas Light, Stuart E. Johnson, Alireza Nader, Angel Rabasa, and Harun Dogo, *Imported Oil and U.S. National Security*, Santa Monica, Calif.: RAND Corporation, MG-838-USCC, 2009.

RAND Project AIR FORCE

RAND Project AIR FORCE (PAF), a division of the RAND Corporation, is the U.S. Air Force's federally funded research and development center for studies and analyses. PAF provides the Air Force with independent analyses of policy alternatives affecting the development, employment, combat readiness, and support of current and future air, space, and cyber forces. Research is conducted in four programs: Force Modernization and Employment; Manpower, Personnel, and Training; Resource Management; and Strategy and Doctrine.

Additional information about PAF is available on our website:
http://www.rand.org/paf/

Contents

Figures

Tables

Summary

Nine nations border the Gulf of Guinea: Cote D'Ivoire, Ghana, Togo, Benin, Nigeria, Cameroon, São Tome and Principe, Equatorial Guinea, and Gabon. Certain of these nations important sources of petroleum for the world market, producing a total of 2.9 million barrels per day, which is 3.5 percent of global petroleum production. For logistical reasons, the main destinations of petroleum exports from the Gulf of Guinea are the United States and Europe. Tanker transit to refineries on the East and Gulf coasts of the United States and to Europe is relatively short and has the added advantage of not passing through vulnerable choke points.

The nations of the Gulf of Guinea control roughly the same percentage of proven reserves, although, because large portions of the Gulf's offshore waters are underexplored, reserve estimates may well understate available resources.

The largest producer by far in the region is Nigeria, which produced 2.2 million of the Gulf of Guinea's 2.9 million barrels per day in 2009. Nigeria also has 37.2 billion barrels of proven reserves, the lion's share of the gulf's total proven reserves of 42.9 billion barrels. We estimate total recoverable petroleum resources at roughly triple this amount.

The oil infrastructure in Nigeria is not well secured, and this has two unfortunate consequences:

- The existing infrastructure is underproducing. In 2009, direct attacks on the petroleum infrastructure and pipeline damage stemming from oil theft in the Niger delta shut down an average of 1.1 million barrels per day of production.
- Investments in oil-producing infrastructure are lower than they would be in a secure environment.

It is in the interests of the United States, as well as other oil-importing nations, to encourage greater production and investment that would raise petroleum output in Nigeria and in the other Gulf of Guinea nations with crude oil reserves. Specifically, greater production from this region adds to diversity of supply and weakens the ability of the core nations of the Organization of Petroleum Exporting Countries cartel to maintain high prices.

Until recently, most production in Nigeria has been on land, in the Niger Delta region. Production facilities have tended to be modest in size and widely dispersed. Much of the terrain has heavy foliage cover. In this environment, aviation forces can make only a limited contribution to the security of the oil-producing infrastructure.

In the past decade, however, production has been moving offshore, and by next year, approximately 60 percent of Nigerian production will be from offshore facilities. Installations that tap the offshore fields tend to be larger and have more output, so it is cost-effective to invest sizable resources to protect them. Second, offshore installations are readily visible from the air, yielding a potentially powerful role for aviation forces. Offshore petroleum development is also taking place in other gulf nations, including Ghana, Benin, Cote D'Ivoire, and Equatorial Guinea.

This growing investment in offshore petroleum production provides an opportunity for the U.S. Air Force to contribute to improved regional energy security. Its primary contribution would be to partner with the air force of Nigeria, the region's largest oil exporter, to build its capacity to secure the oil-producing infrastructure from attack. Specifically, we investigated capabilities that would deter or, if necessary, defeat attacks on oil-producing installations by providing a rapid response capability to interdict the perpetrators.

There are three areas where partnership capacity building could provide a high payoff:

- a command and control center that could receive alerts of an attack on an installation and coordinate a response
- a surveillance capability that could locate and track attackers
- a rapid response transport capability to fly security forces to interdict the attackers.

The report includes an analysis of potential operations, which frames what it would take to achieve a basic level of the above capabilities. Such a demonstrated capability to defeat attackers can be expected to strongly deter groups considering an attack on offshore oil-producing installations.

These three capabilities are core capabilities of the U.S. Air Force and are not the kind of capabilities that could readily be turned against the population—always a consideration in building partner capacity.

There are three obstacles to partnering that the team identified:

1. The Nigerian Air Force has a relatively low level of pilot training. The initial training and assistance would have to aim for a very modest initial capability in each area and build from there.
2. The Nigerian government has in the past been reluctant to partner with the U.S. military. Initial capacity building might have to focus on noncombat missions, such as search and rescue or medical evacuation. These missions demand most of the same basic pilot skills as those described above for defeating an attack.
3. The Nigerian government suffers from corruption, which will make partnering with its military difficult. This indicates adopting a strategy that begins modestly and being prepared to intensify the capacity building in the event that corruption recedes.

Although there are challenges, Nigeria still has good reason to partner with the United States. Increasing the security of Nigerian oil infrastructure would increase oil production, and the vast majority of the country's wealth lies in its hydrocarbon sector. Therefore, Nigeria should be willing to work with the United States. Nevertheless, there are alternatives. One is to work first with other nations in the region, such as Ghana, where governance is considerably better. As the U.S. Air Force gains experience in building capacity with these partners, it could draw on its lessons learned and best practices to partner with other countries, including Nigeria, should governance improve.

Acknowledgments

Numerous individuals assisted and contributed to this research. We especially gained from our discussions with Lt Col Hap Harlow, USAF, U.S. Africa Command Strategy Division; Lt Col John Yocum, Maj Matthew L. May, and Maj Demetrius Mizell, all with the 17th Air Force; and Hunter Hustus in his role as Political Advisor, USAF Africa. Lt Col Jordan Thomas, AF/A5XS, who monitored our progress, also provided useful guidance throughout.

We also benefited from discussions with and, in some cases, analyses from RAND colleagues, including Howard Shatz and Stacie Pettyjohn. Three students from the Pardee RAND Graduate School—Tewodaj Mengistu, Xiao Wang, and Yashodhara Rana—and Marco Overhaus of the Transatlantic Post-Doc Fellowship for International Relations and Security program provided research assistance. The authors are grateful to Richard Betts of Columbia University and Frank Camm at RAND, whose rigorous reviews strengthened and improved this document.

During the course of our research, we met with senior-level representatives of international oil companies that are investing and operating in the Gulf of Guinea. To encourage frank and open discussion during these meetings, they were held on a not-for-attribution basis. These discussions proved to be highly valuable to our research.

Abbreviations

AFRICOM	United States Africa Command
bcm	billion cubic meters
bpd	barrels per day
C3	command, control, and communications
DoD	Department of Defense
EIA	Energy Information Administration
FPSO	floating production, storage, and offloading
ICG	International Crisis Group
IISS	International Institute for Strategic Studies
JTF	joint task force
JTIC	Jane's Terrorism Insurgency Centre
LNG	liquefied natural gas
MEND	Movement for the Emancipation of the Niger Delta
NDV	Niger Delta Vigilantes
NNPC	Nigerian National Petroleum Corporation
OPEC	Organization of the Petroleum Exporting Countries
PAF	Project AIR FORCE
RTT	rapid tactical transport
tcm	trillion cubic meters
USAF	U.S. Air Force

Prologue

This volume reports on exploratory research undertaken as part of broader study directed at energy security and how it affects U.S. Air Force (USAF) planning. That broader study examined the world oil market, how developments in that market might affect "wholesale" supplies of jet fuel, and what measures the Air Force might take to protect itself against high fuel prices and supply disruptions, as documented in Bartis, 2012. To better examine the potential role of the Air Force in promoting international energy security, we conducted three exploratory studies. The first addresses the Caspian and Turkey and is documented in Weiss et al., 2012. The second addresses the sea lanes from Hormuz to Asia and is documented in Henry et al., 2012. The last, documented here, focuses on the Gulf of Guinea. This prologue presents an overall summary of the findings of the broader study on energy security, so that readers will be able to place the current volume in that context.

The World Oil Market

Global demand for liquid fuels is about 87 million barrels per day (bpd). Presently, over 98 percent of this demand is met by petroleum products derived from crude oil and, to a much smaller degree, liquid hydrocarbons that are coproduced with natural gas. Over half of global crude oil production enters the international oil trade.

As is the case with many other commodities, oil prices are subject to large variations. For petroleum, price volatility is especially pronounced for three reasons:

1. It takes a fairly long time to bring new production online in response to price signals—generally at least six years and often much longer.
2. Once new production is brought online, the marginal costs of continuing production are fairly low.
3. Over the short term, petroleum demand is fairly unresponsive to prices.

These three factors account for the persistent high petroleum prices during most of the 1970s and early 1980s and the 17 years of low prices beginning in 1985. The low petroleum prices during the late 1980s and 1990s resulted in what, in retrospect, turned out to be an underinvestment in new petroleum production, leading to historically high crude oil prices during 2007 and 2008.

Complicating this structural picture of the world petroleum market are two major institutional problems. The first is the existence of an international oil cartel, the Organization of the Petroleum Exporting Countries (OPEC). OPEC has a strong interest in keeping world crude oil prices high and reducing price volatility. The history of oil prices since 1973, however, shows that OPEC has had mixed success with both objectives. In fact, the net result of OPEC's existence may be increased crude oil price volatility, since OPEC's attempts to maintain high oil prices, when prices are already high, tend to promote additional investment in new oil production in nations, including some members of OPEC, that do not conform to OPEC's production quotas.

The second institutional problem stems from the location of the world's petroleum resources. While most of the world's conventional petroleum resources are located in nations astride the Persian Gulf, there are also appreciable resources in many other locations. But nearly all the major oil-exporting nations outside the Persian Gulf, and a few inside, suffer from governance problems that seriously impede investment in additional productive capacity. The notable exceptions are Canada and Norway. By presenting a barrier to investment in petroleum (and natural gas) production, governance shortfalls have made world oil prices more volatile and higher than they would otherwise be. For example, considering just two countries, Iraq and Nigeria, continuing conflict is keeping daily production millions of barrels below what their combined resource base is able to support. In most of the other important oil-exporting countries, governance shortfalls center on corruption, the lack of the rule of law, and persistent violations of human rights.

Responding to the Market

The first volume of this series examines the measures that the Air Force, and more broadly, the U.S. Department of Defense (DoD), can take in response to the structural and institutional conditions that characterize the world petroleum market. While DoD is one of the world's largest fuel users, its consumption of about 340,000 bpd is a small fraction (less than 0.5 percent) of global petroleum demand. Considering that U.S. domestic petroleum production is about 7.5 million bpd, and that an additional 3 million bpd of secure supplies are imported from Canada and Mexico, we can find no credible scenario in which the military would be unable to access the 340,000 bpd of fuel that it needs to defend the nation.

While DoD and the services will have access to the wholesale fuel supplies that they require, the price for those supplies may be high. As fuel consumers, DoD and the services have only one effective option for dealing with high petroleum prices: reducing overall petroleum fuel use. This can be accomplished by purchasing equipment and adopting maneuver schemes that are more energy efficient and, in the short term, by implementing energy conservation measures to reduce petroleum use. We also found that alternative fuels do not offer DoD a way to appreciably reduce fuel costs.[1]

Promoting Energy Security

USAF plays an important and productive role in the world oil market, not as a consumer but rather as one of the armed services of the United States. The armed services are the backbone of

---

[1]   This finding was published in a recent RAND report, *Alternative Fuels for Military Applications* (Bartis and Van Bibber, 2011), and revalidated as part of the research reported herein.

the U.S. national security policy that ensures access to the energy supplies of the Persian Gulf and the stability and security of key friendly states in the region. Moreover, the U.S. Navy, by its global presence, ensures freedom of passage in the sea lanes that are crucial to international trade in petroleum and natural gas.

Can more be done? Is there a productive role for the Air Force in further promoting energy security? To answer these questions, we conducted three exploratory studies focusing on (1) Nigeria and other potential oil-exporting countries in the Gulf of Guinea, (2) the Caspian oil- and gas-exporting nations and Turkey, and (3) the sea lanes from Hormuz to Asia. We purposely selected topic areas outside of the Middle East because the U.S. military is already active in the Persian Gulf and the Strait of Hormuz. Additionally, energy security issues within the Middle East have been well studied.

The analyses reported in the three volumes of exploratory studies led us to conclude that there is a role for the Air Force but that important caveats apply. In nations where security shortfalls impede hydrocarbon production or transport, current and future USAF capabilities in building partnership capacity offer security improvements that could promote greater production of petroleum and natural gas resources. Notable examples of nations where security shortfalls are significantly impeding investment and production are Nigeria and Iraq. While we did not examine the situation in Iraq, our review of opportunities to build partnership capacity in Nigeria and other nations bordering the Gulf of Guinea suggests that any efforts to build military partnerships in this region must consider broader U.S. goals, especially the risks that U.S.-provided military capabilities might be applied to local civilian populations. While there are signs of improved governance in Nigeria, these considerations suggest that Ghana may be a more attractive partner.

In examining the Caspian Region, the major energy supply challenge for current and future energy flows stems from the region's need for significant upstream investment, the lack of a well-developed export infrastructure, and Russia's desire to determine how the region's energy resources are developed. Although the Russian invasion of Georgia in 2008 did not directly target energy infrastructure, most export routes for oil and natural gas from Azerbaijan to Turkey were interrupted for several weeks because of the combination of precautionary shutdowns and an apparent sabotage attack inside Turkey. With regard to the remaining nations in the Caspian region, we found that direct threats to the security of the energy infrastructure are being fairly well addressed, especially considering the current low threat level.

Turkey appears as a special case because of its geostrategic location, status as a North Atlantic Treaty Organization (NATO) member, and long-time relationship with USAF. Kurdish terrorists have been able to execute numerous successful attacks on oil pipelines traversing eastern Turkey. The pace of attacks against energy-related targets will cause investors to weigh pipeline security risks when considering the large investments that will be required if Turkey is to realize its goal of becoming an energy hub between Europe and both the Caspian and the Middle East. Another important Turkish energy transit issue is the oil tanker traffic through the Bosporus Strait. From the Turkish perspective, concerns center on limiting heavy tanker traffic and transit delays in the Bosporus and coping with the potential damage from a major oil spill. From the oil industry perspective, transit security concerns center on a terrorist attack or navigation accident that might block tanker passage for many months. Considering its state of development and military capabilities, Turkey certainly has the wherewithal to address pipeline attacks and the concerns regarding the Bosporus. However, USAF could play a productive, albeit limited, role in promoting technology transfer and best practices on infrastructure protection, with the main motivation being strengthening the U.S. and USAF relationship with Turkey.

Another potential role for USAF is in assisting the U.S. Navy in sea-lane protection, which is the subject of the third volume of this series of technical reports. Asia's sea lines of communication are a growing security concern because of the increasing dependence of rapidly expanding Asian economies on imported energy sources—oil and natural gas. Unfortunately, regional security mechanisms have not kept pace and are no longer commensurate with the rise in the region's significance.

On this topic, our first major finding is that a joint approach, in which USAF provides meaningful assistance to the Navy, offers a more efficient and effective application of U.S. defense assets. By capitalizing on USAF-Navy interdependencies, a joint approach would lay a foundation for addressing more-strategic concerns, including the overall USAF role in assuring access to the global commons, and the collaborative development of an interdependent force posture. Our second, and more significant, finding is that overall U.S. interests are best served by a multinational approach to the protection of the energy sea lanes to Asia. This approach provides a much better mechanism for addressing potentially serious threats that might arise if one or more of the countries along the sea-lane fails or goes rogue. Additionally, multinational cooperation in sea lines of communication protection provides a means of dampening the lingering tensions and simmering disputes that prevail within Asia. From the USAF perspective, a multinational approach provides new opportunities for interaction, building partnerships, and assuring access.

CHAPTER ONE

Introduction

Nigeria and its neighbors in the Gulf of Guinea are important sources of petroleum for the Atlantic Basin (Figure 1.1).[1] In 2010, production was about 3.1 million barrels per day (bpd), the bulk of which was exported (Energy Information Administration [EIA], 2011). This amount is 3.5 percent of the global output of liquid fuels.[2] Proven reserves of crude oil in this region represent 3.3 percent of the global total. With large untapped resources of oil and natural gas, these nations have the potential to expand their output significantly. For example, an oil field estimated to hold well over 2 billion barrels of crude oil has recently been found off the

Figure 1.1
The Nine Gulf of Guinea Nations and Capital Cities

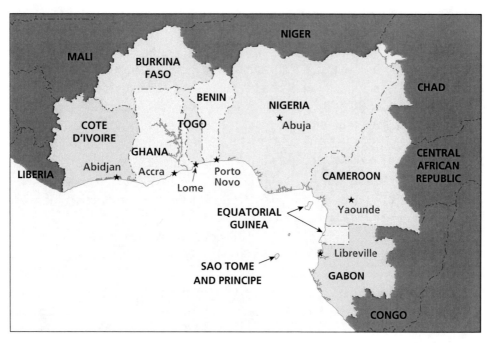

RAND TR1144z4-1.1

---

[1]   Consistent with international conventions, we consider the following nations as belonging to the Gulf of Guinea: Cote D'Ivoire, Ghana, Togo, Benin, Nigeria, Cameroon, São Tome and Principe, Equatorial Guinea, and Gabon (International Hydrographic Organization, 1953).

[2]   Liquid fuels include petroleum products derived from crude oil; natural gas plant liquids; and biofuels, most notably ethanol.

coast of Ghana, indicating that the proven reserves in the western part of the Gulf of Guinea could increase significantly over the next few years.

As a major energy-consuming country, the United States stands to benefit from diversification of energy supplies, which helps lower energy prices and strengthens energy security. In the short term, the nation's interest is to ensure reliable production and secure transit of oil from the region up to the full potential of its existing infrastructure. Stable production in the Gulf of Guinea would lessen price volatility and reduce the magnitude of price shocks in the global market for crude oil. Over the longer term, the United States would like to see the region attract the investment required to expand production both by tapping the considerable proven energy reserves and by exploring promising new areas. Expanded production would lessen global dependence on Persian Gulf suppliers and thereby exert downward pressure on crude oil prices.

Advancing these interests requires a stable operating environment, and here the picture is mixed. Nigeria, by far the largest producer, suffers from attacks on and theft from its energy-producing infrastructure. The shut-in (lost) production in 2009 was estimated to be 1.1 million bpd (EIA, 2010). This estimate covers losses where investments have already been made. While figures of forgone investment are difficult to come by, conversations with officials of major American oil companies revealed that, when making decisions about where to invest in exploration and development, the uncertain security environment in Nigeria and certain other nations in the Gulf of Guinea makes investment there less attractive relative to other regions.

The remaining hydrocarbon production in the Gulf of Guinea centers on three nations: Gabon, Equatorial Guinea, and Ghana. For both Gabon and Equatorial Guinea, production has been declining in recent years, despite high oil prices. In contrast to Nigeria, the petroleum and natural gas production infrastructure is fairly secure. Nonetheless, the investment environment, especially in Equatorial Guinea, does suffer from shortfalls in governance, such as corruption and uneven application of the law. In 2011, Ghana's production jumped from a few thousand bpd to over 80,000 bpd, thanks to oil discoveries made in 2007. Prospects for continued production growth in Ghana are good, albeit somewhat uncertain. In Ghana's favor is its stable and effective government.

This report examines potential roles for the U.S. Air Force in promoting energy security in the Gulf of Guinea. Our emphasis is primarily on Nigeria, since Nigeria is the dominant producer in the region and continues to suffer from attacks on its production infrastructure.

Chapter Two surveys hydrocarbon resources and production in the Gulf of Guinea. The next two chapters focus on Nigeria. Chapter Three outlines the threats to Nigeria's hydrocarbon security, which include pipeline sabotage, oil theft, assaults on installations and personnel, and the kidnapping for ransom of petroleum company employees. Chapter Four provides an overview of Nigeria's armed forces, catalogs the equipment they use, and discusses their shortcomings in training and equipment maintenance, and relates the history of corruption in their leadership.

Chapter Five examines the challenges to and opportunities for partnering with the Nigerian armed forces to improve their capacity to protect their hydrocarbon infrastructure. Our research and extensive interviews with Department of State personnel; U.S. military personnel, including staff at U.S. Africa Command (AFRICOM) headquarters and the 17th Air Force (the Air Force component that has been supporting AFRICOM); representatives of petroleum companies operating in the Gulf of Guinea; and other regional experts helped us identify three opportunities for capacity-building partnerships in the Gulf of Guinea.

Two options are put forward for a capacity-building partnership with the Nigerian Air Force. The first would be a modest program focused on developing maritime search and rescue, medical evacuation, and exclusive economic zone enforcement. The second option would focus directly on protecting the offshore energy infrastructure by building capacity in airborne surveillance, rapid tactical transport (RTT), and command, control, and communications (C3). The third option would focus on building the capacity of Ghana's Air Force to protect its emerging offshore energy infrastructure.

Appendix A presents a parametric analysis of potential operations by framing the basic level of capability for responding to an assault on Nigeria's offshore energy infrastructure.

Appendix B is an overview of the perspectives of the representatives of international oil companies that we interviewed over the course of the project. These interviews provide an important perspective on the threats facing Nigeria's oil sector and were important in shaping our recommendations for how the U.S. Air Force can help Nigeria address these threats.

CHAPTER TWO

Hydrocarbon Resources and Production

The Gulf of Guinea holds 43 billion barrels of proven oil reserves, but the region is underexplored, and geologists estimate the total recoverable petroleum resources to be roughly triple this amount.[1] As Table 2.1 illustrates, the proven reserves are concentrated in Nigeria. Limited exploration beyond the Niger Delta is very likely the primary reason for the very low proven reserve levels that have been recorded for the other nations in the region. We anticipate substantial growth in the proven reserves of countries in other parts of the Gulf as exploration progresses from 2011 to 2021.

Likewise, Nigeria is recorded as holding nearly all the proven natural gas resources. Its 5.3 trillion cubic meters (tcm)—the energy equivalent of about 35 billion barrels of crude oil—of proven reserves make this the eighth largest natural gas reserve in the world. For the region, an estimate of roughly 15 tcm total recoverable natural gas is indicated.

In 2010, overall petroleum production in the Gulf of Guinea averaged 3.1 million bpd. The region itself uses 0.5 million bpd, leaving net exports of about 2.6 million bpd. As shown in Table 2.2, Nigeria is the dominant petroleum producer, and is likely to remain so over the next few decades, although we anticipate that production from other Gulf of Guinea nations will increase.

The region produced about 37 billion cubic meters (bcm) of marketable natural gas in 2010, the energy equivalent of about 650,000 bpd of crude oil. As with petroleum, Nigeria is

Table 2.1
Gulf of Guinea Proven Energy Reserves

	Petroleum (bbs)	Natural Gas (trillion m^3)
Cameroon	0.20	0.1
Equatorial Guinea	1.70	<0.1
Gabon	3.70	<0.1
Ghana	0.02	1
Nigeria	37.20	5.3
Other Gulf of Guinea	0.10	<0.2
Total	42.92	5.5

SOURCES: BP, 2011; EIA, 2011.

---

[1] *Recoverable resources* include proven reserves, reserve growth, and undiscovered resources. For both petroleum and natural gas, we assumed a reserve growth of 70 percent of proven reserves (see Ahlbrandt, 2004, p. 569; Charpentier, 2004, p. 250). For undiscovered resources, we used the F50 recovery estimates (see U.S. Geological Survey, 2003).

Table 2.2
2010 Production of Petroleum and Natural Gas

	Petroleum (million bpd)	Natural Gas (dry bcm per year)
Cameroon	0.070	<0.1
Cote d'Ivoire	0.040	1.6
Equatorial Guinea	0.320	6.7
Gabon	0.230	<0.1
Ghana	0.007	0
Nigeria	2.460	29.0
Total	3.120	37.4

SOURCE: EIA, 2011.

the dominant regional producer of natural gas, at about 75 percent. Most natural gas in the region is produced as a byproduct of crude oil and is therefore sensitive to the same security conditions. As with oil, these conditions have deterred investment in new production and have reduced actual production levels to substantially below existing capacity. However, the primary limitation on marketable production has been the lack of infrastructure for local use of natural gas, such as natural gas–fired electric power plants, and the gas pipelines required to bring natural gas to regional demand centers and global markets. Much of current production is vented, flared, or reinjected into the petroleum deposit.

With the exception of Nigeria and Equatorial Guinea, natural gas production is used to meet domestic needs. Nigeria and Equatorial Guinea export about 15 bcm in the form of liquefied natural gas (LNG). We expect natural gas exports to increase significantly as Nigeria and Equatorial Guinea increase their capacities for LNG production. LNG can be and has been shipped long distances economically to reach markets in the United States, Europe, and Asia.

Nigeria is a large country, twice the size of California. With over 150 million inhabitants, it leads Africa in both population and population density. Because of the magnitude of its oil production, Nigeria is the one country in the region where fluctuations in output can have significantly affect global energy markets.[2] Considering the country's regional dominance in proven reserves, this situation is likely to continue. This report, therefore, focuses primarily on opportunities for and impediments to working with Nigeria to build its capacity to secure its energy-producing infrastructure.

Oil

The first significant discovery of oil in Nigeria occurred in 1956. Realizing the value of its oil reserves, the government nationalized the oil industry in 1971 by creating a national oil company, now named the Nigerian National Petroleum Corporation (NNPC). NNPC holds a majority share in all Nigerian oil production projects. It typically works with foreign oil

---

[2]   The 2008 attack on Shell's offshore Bonga facility had this effect (Yergin, 2008, pp. 2–3). Bonga lies 75 miles off the coast and has a capacity of more than 200,000 bpd ("Nigeria Attack Stops . . . ," 2008). In June 2008, militants in speedboats attacked a vessel used for production storage and offloading and kidnapped an American oil worker. The shutdown of Bonga alone cut Nigeria's total oil output by 10 percent ("Nigerian Attack Closes . . . ," 2008). Speculators in oil futures appear to respond strongly to attacks on energy infrastructure and tend to increase the near-term effects of any resultant production loss (Giroux and Hilpert, 2009).

companies through joint ventures to develop fields and produce crude oil (International Crisis Group [ICG], 2006, p. 19). The major foreign producers in Nigeria are Shell, Chevron, Exxon-Mobil, Total, and Eni/Agip. For the most part, production yields a light, sweet crude, which refiners use for making gasoline. About 40 percent of Nigerian production is exported to the United States (EIA, 2010).

Nigeria's oil sector has become the nation's most profitable industry and dominates the economy, as well as the landscape of the Niger Delta (see Figures 2.1 and 2.2). But as in many other oil-exporting nations, the government has done little to diversify Nigeria's economy. For example, despite the abundance of crude oil, Nigeria has inadequate refining capacity and must import almost 85 percent of its refined petroleum products (EIA, 2010).

Until 1993, oil exploration and production were limited to hundreds of small fields located in the inland areas and swamps of the Niger Delta and shallow waters near the shore (NNPC, 2010b).

Recent technological advances have enabled the development of large, deep-water (>400 m) oil fields further out in the Gulf of Guinea. In 2005, Shell's Bonga field, Nigeria's first deep-water oil field, began operating 120 km off the coast and now produces over 200,000 bpd of crude oil. The Bonga field was soon followed by the Erha field, operated by ExxonMobil; the Agbami field, operated by Chevron; and the Akpo field, operated by Total (Arab Press Service, 2009; Mbiriri, 2009).

In some cases, oil produced offshore is stored offshore and loaded onto tankers using facilities colocated with the production wells (see Figures 2.3 and 2.4), thereby bypassing the need for pipelines and onshore storage and loading terminals.

Figure 2.1
The Location of Nigeria's Oil-Producing Region

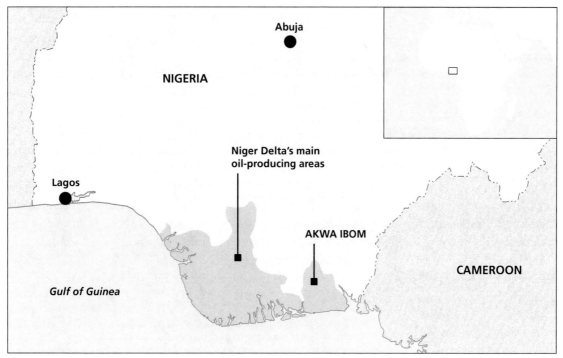

Figure 2.2
Oil and Gas Fields in the Niger Delta Region

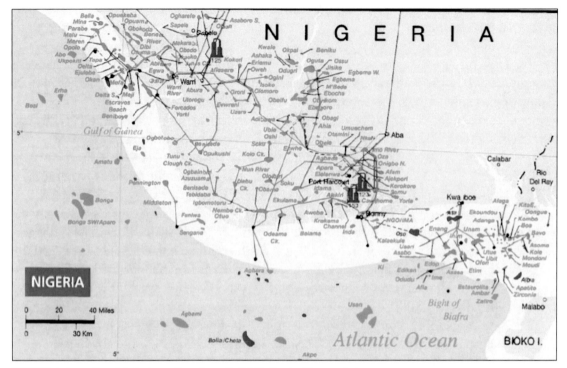

SOURCE: International Petroleum Encyclopedia 2009. Used with permission.
NOTE: Green areas = oil fields. Red areas = gas fields. Purple symbols = large refineries. Black dots = oil terminals.
Solid lines = major pipelines. Dotted lines = planned pipelines.
RAND TR1144z4-2.2

Explorations of the deep-water areas near Nigeria have met with great success. Nigeria's deep-water output ranks fourth in the world, exceeded only by the deep-water production of the United States, Brazil, and Angola (Sandrea and Sandrea, 2010). Moreover, the deep off-shore area is likely to continue to grow in importance to Nigeria and to other nations in the Gulf of Guinea (Barkindo, 2007; Tuttle, Charpentier, and Brownfield, 1999).

Natural Gas

For the most part, natural gas is a byproduct of crude oil production in Nigeria. Only a few reservoirs produce natural gas exclusively. Until the 1980s, coproduced gas was dismissed as useless because there were few ways to store or transport it economically to users (Chevron, 2010; Walker, 2009). In many cases, oil companies flared or burned off this coproduced gas.

This situation has been changing. Demand in Nigeria and nearby nations for natural gas has grown, and a global market for LNG has emerged.[3] Presently, about 15 bcm per year of natural gas is exported in the form of LNG.[4] All Nigerian LNG is produced in a single large production facility located on Bonny Island and owned by NNPC, Shell, Total, and ENI. Additional facilities are in planning or construction, but whether and when new LNG facilities

---

[3]   LNG is produced by cooling natural gas to a temperature slightly below −160°C so that it becomes a liquid. This liquid can be transported over long distances in specially designed cryogenic ships to facilities that can regasify the LNG.

[4]   This is the energy equivalent of about 270,000 bpd of crude oil.

Figure 2.3
Chevron Floating Production, Storage, and Offloading (FPSO) Vessel Operating in the Agbami Oil Field

SOURCE: Chevron Corporation. Used with permission.
RAND *TR1144z4-2.3*

will become operational in Nigeria depends on developments in the global LNG market and the security situation in Nigeria.

The new West African Gas Pipeline has further boosted Nigerian natural gas exports. A joint venture of Chevron, NNPC, Shell, and three local companies, this undersea pipeline can deliver Nigerian gas to Benin, Togo, and Ghana. Initial capacity is about 2 bcm per year. Current shipments primarily support electric power generation in the receiving nations.

Chevron and NNPC are also developing a multibillion-dollar gas-to-liquids facility at Escravos to produce about 33,000 bpd of liquid fuels, primarily diesel and naphtha.[5] The inability of the government to ensure security appears to have caused the schedule for initial production from this gas-to-liquids facility to slip from 2010 to 2013 (EIA, 2010; Chevron, 2011).

As a result of the changes that made natural gas production profitable, the Nigerian government put forward a gas master plan in 2009 that aims to eliminate natural gas flaring, to increase the country's extremely low electricity production by developing gas-fired power plants, and to increase natural gas exports (Ukpohor, 2009).

Also in accordance with the gas master plan, the governments of Nigeria, Niger, and Algeria agreed in 2009 to develop a 2,500-mile gas pipeline across the Sahara, with a terminus

---

[5]   Naphtha is a mixture of hydrocarbons that can be processed to produce gasoline. It can also serve as a feedstock for the production of petrochemicals.

Figure 2.4
Onshore and Offshore Oil Production in the Niger Delta

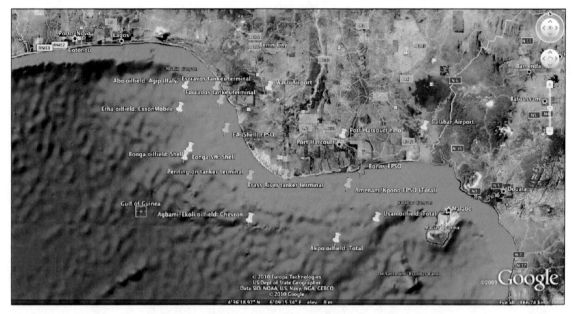

SOURCE: Copyright 2010 Google; copyright 2010 Europa Technologies.
NOTE: Yellow pins = known locations of oil fields. Green pins = FPSO facilities and tanker terminals.
RAND *TR1144z4-2.4*

on Algeria's Mediterranean coast. The planned pipeline would enable Nigeria to significantly increase its exports of natural gas to European markets. Moreover, the Trans-Sahara Gas Pipeline would provide the European Union an opportunity to diversify its energy resources and thereby make it less reliant on Russian natural gas. Nevertheless, questions remain about whether the pipeline can successfully be constructed and secured, given the inadequate security in Nigeria, Niger, and Algeria (Watkins, 2009; Fabiani, 2009).

Other Nations in the Gulf of Guinea

This section briefly reviews the hydrocarbon production trends in Gabon, Equatorial Guinea, and Ghana. Although the levels are well below those of Nigeria, oil exports dominate the economies of both Gabon and Equatorial Guinea. Ghana, one of the best governed countries in sub-Saharan Africa, saw a dramatic increase in production during 2011. These three nations, plus Nigeria, are the only countries in the Gulf of Guinea that have near-term prospects of producing over 250,000 bpd.

Motivated by the recent finds in Ghana, a few petroleum companies are actively looking for oil off the shores of Benin, Togo, and Cote d'Ivoire. Exploratory activities are also occurring in the limited offshore acreage Cameroon controls. But in late 2011, exploratory work in these four nations was still in the early stages, and no new finds had been reported.

Gabon

Gabon is a nation of 1.5 million occupying an area roughly the size of Colorado. As of 2011, oil revenues made up more than 40 percent of the nation's gross domestic product. Oil has been produced in Gabon for over 50 years. Production ramped up in the late 1960s and reached a peak of 365,000 bpd in 1996. Since then, oil production has declined to the current level of about 230,000 bpd, despite much higher world oil prices (BP, 2011).

In Gabon, natural gas is an oil coproduct, but very little of it has been marketed. In response to a ban on gas flaring, companies are, for the most part, reinjecting gas into oil fields, pending the deployment of infrastructure that would allow greater domestic use, such as power generation, and possibly gas exports in the form of LNG (de Zardain, 2011).

Whether Gabon's petroleum production is doomed to a slow decline remains highly uncertain. Companies operating in Gabon have reported recent discoveries, but the new finds, both on and off shore, are fairly small. There is speculation that massive quantities of oil exist in deep offshore deposits, similar to those recently discovered off Ghana, and in ultradeep offshore deposits similar to those in "presalt" deposits off the Brazilian coast (de Zardain, 2011). Exploration is occurring or planned (Harvest Natural Resources, 2011; Petrobras, 2011).

We found no evidence that security shortfalls are impeding production or investment in hydrocarbon production in Gabon. Additional protective capabilities may be appropriate if and when large investments are made in far-offshore oilfield development. Otherwise, energy security issues in Gabon are unlikely to motivate a role for the U.S. Air Force in building Gabon's capabilities to protect the portions of the hydrocarbon supply chain that lie in its territory.

Equatorial Guinea

Equatorial Guinea is small and sparsely populated—about the size of Maryland but with roughly one-tenth of the population. The nation includes islands, notably Bioko Island off the coast of Cameroon and Annobon Island off the coast of Gabon, that allow Equatorial Guinea to control an extensive amount of offshore oil and gas acreage.[6] In 2011, oil and gas development and sales dwarfed all other economic activity (U.S. Department of State, 2011a).

Despite extensive reserves, the development of Equatorial Guinea's hydrocarbon resources did not begin until the 1990s. Petroleum production peaked in 2005 at 375,000 bpd and has since slowly declined, with 2010 production at about 320,000 bpd. Production of marketable quantities of natural gas began in 2002 (EIA, 2011). In 2007, Marathon Oil Corporation and partners opened the Alba LNG plant on Bioko Island, thereby allowing natural gas to be exported. About a quarter of current production is used domestically, and the remainder is exported as LNG.

All oil and gas production and exploration activities occur offshore. The long-term outlook for petroleum and natural gas production in Equatorial Guinea will depend on that nation's ability to attract foreign companies that have the know-how and financial resources to find and extract oil and natural gas resources located in deep offshore deposits. According to the U.S. Department of State, "the business climate [in Equatorial Guinea] remains difficult. Application of the laws remains selective. Corruption among officials is widespread, and

---

[6]   Both Gabon and Equatorial Guinea claim sovereignty over three small, uninhabited islands off the coast of Gabon. As of this writing, the United Nations is mediating this dispute. Meanwhile, both nations have agreed on joint exploration of their contested offshore waters, pending resolution of this dispute (Yoon, 2009).

many business deals are concluded under nontransparent circumstances" (U.S. Department of State, 2011a). These same problems were in place during the rapid buildup of production that occurred since 2001. Whether their persistence will deter the greater investments required for deep drilling remains uncertain. A further impediment is Equatorial Guinea's severe short-comings in human rights and political freedom (U.S. Department of State, 2011b).

We did not find evidence that security shortfalls in Equatorial Guinea are impeding production. As with Gabon, a shift to hydrocarbon deposits further offshore might require additional protective capabilities that airborne assets can provide. Any consideration of future U.S. Air Force cooperation with the defense forces of Equatorial Guinea will likely include a review of that nation's progress in controlling corruption and protecting human rights.

Ghana

Ghana stands out as one of the best governed nations in Africa. It is slightly larger than Minnesota. With about 25 million inhabitants, it ranks second in population among the nations of the Gulf of Guinea. For decades, Ghana has produced a small amount of oil—a few thousand bpd—but not enough to satisfy domestic demand. This situation abruptly changed in December 2010 when the first well from the Jubilee oil field began production. During 2011, that field produced an average of 80,000 bpd (Tullow Oil, 2011). Production is anticipated to reach 120,000 bpd in 2012, with the ultimate goal being about 250,000 bpd of oil and about 2.5 bcm per year of natural gas.

Jubilee is a significant oil field. Proven reserves are 490 million barrels (Tullow Oil, 2010). Recoverable resources may be well over 1 billion barrels. Oil has also been found in a number of other fields off the coast of Ghana. In 2011, these deposits were being evaluated to determine their oil and natural gas production potential. So far, Ghana has been able to attract expertise and investment from a number of oil exploration and production firms. If the current exploration program plays out favorably, Ghana could be producing more than 0.5 million bpd in the next decade. Much higher production rates are possible but not yet supported by publicly available information.

Our research did not reveal any imminent threats to the infrastructure and persons associated with Ghana's recent increase in petroleum production. The government of Ghana does recognize the need to strengthen existing security agencies to meet the challenges of this growing industry. Toward this end, the Ghana Minister for Defense, Lt. Gen. Joseph Henry Smith (ret.), established a National Petroleum Security Coordinating Committee, effective January 2011 (Zaney, 2011).

We discussed this concern further during a not-for-attribution conversation with a senior official of the government of Ghana in March 2011. In particular, we were informed of the government's deep concern about potential threats to the offshore oil and gas infrastructure and the current capacity of Ghana to deter or respond to offshore attacks. Motivating this concern is Ghana's proximity to Nigeria, where groups have attacked offshore infrastructure, as further discussed in the next chapter.

CHAPTER THREE

The Security Threat to Nigerian Hydrocarbon Production

Security problems center on oil bunkering (tapping a pipeline to steal oil), attacks on the petroleum infrastructure, and kidnappings of oil personnel. These problems have reduced output of and restrained investment in Nigeria's energy sector. One notable attack, in January 2006 on a Shell facility in the Niger Delta, caused a 250,000-bpd drop in Nigerian oil production and a temporary spike in world oil prices (Junger, 2007). The Air Force itself cannot counter bunkering or kidnapping.

Both threats are inherently deterrence problems that rely on local information and intelligence that only the Nigerian government can gather. The options for partnering with Nigeria, therefore, seek to bolster these skills.

The Niger Delta is approximately 70,000 km^2 of rivers, mangroves, jungles, and swamps. The oil infrastructure is similarly expansive: Shell's operations alone cover more than 30,000 km^2 and include more than 6,000 km of pipelines and flow lines, 90 oil fields, 1,000 producing wells, 72 flow stations, 10 processing plants for coproduced gas, and export terminals at Bonny and Forcados (Shell Nigeria, 2010). The delta's creeks and rivers, which are often covered by dense foliage, offer criminals and militants camouflaged passages for ambushes and escape routes to elude the authorities.[1] The scale of the oil infrastructure and the inhospitable terrain of the Niger Delta pose a particularly challenging security problem.

The lack of security of the delta's oil infrastructure led to production of only 650,000 bpd in 2009—*less* than full capacity. This shut-in production, coupled with losses due to theft and to leakage into the environment associated with theft-associated equipment damage, accounted for an average shortfall of 1.1 million bpd in 2009 (EIA, 2010).

An estimated 150,000 bpd of oil were *stolen* in 2008. Although this is but a small percentage of production, nevertheless the repeated assaults on oil infrastructure have forced oil companies to move steadily farther off shore to pursue deep-water oil fields on the assumption that militants in speedboats would not be able to travel that far. The 2008 attack on the Bonga deep-water oil project tested that assumption. Therefore, regardless of the amount actually stolen, the act alone discourages investment to expand production.

---

[1] Because there are few roads in the Niger Delta, canoes or motor boats are the primary form of transportation (Asuni, 2009a, p. 3).

Political and Social Context for the Petroleum Security Threat

The security threats to petroleum production in Nigeria stem primarily from fundamental internal governance problems.[2] These include ethnic competition and strife, widespread corruption, and the support of violence for political purposes. After decades of British rule, Nigeria was granted independence in 1960. Its national boundaries derived from the colonial structure imposed by the United Kingdom and the other European powers occupying West Africa. In Nigeria's boundaries are hundreds of ethnic groups with little in common, including language. At independence, many of these ethnic groups had no meaningful relationship with one another; some had a long history of antagonism (Human Rights Watch, 2007). There is also a significant religious split, with the north dominated by Islam and the south, Christianity. Lacking a strong national identity and recognizing its historical diversity, Nigerians reorganized their government as a federal republic in 1963.

The move to greater regional autonomy, however, was not sufficient to address the lack of national identity and purpose. Regional and national elections were tainted by fraud and intimidation and led to widespread violence and rioting. Through a series of coups, the military ruled Nigeria between 1966 and 1979 and between 1983 and 1999. Ethnic division persisted during military rule. The Biafran civil war alone claimed over 1 million lives between 1967 and 1970 (Davis, 2009a). Likewise, corruption continued, often centering on the diversion of government revenues received from petroleum production. The second period of military rule was particularly violent and included the cultivation of student gangs to repress calls for democracy at Nigeria's universities.[3]

The restoration of civil rule in 1999 did not end the violence or corruption. The first president was a former Nigerian general, Olusegun Obasanjo, who had previously served as head of state during the period of military rule. In 2007, Umaru Yar'Adua, a Muslim from northern Nigeria, won the presidency in a highly controversial election. Yar'Adua promoted economic development and reform but had limited success in fighting corruption and violence. Soon after his election, he became ill; he died in office in May 2010. For at least the last seven months of his presidency, the severity of Yar'Adua's illness appears to have precluded active leadership of Nigeria.

In February 2010, the Nigerian National Assembly promoted the vice president, Goodluck Jonathan, to acting president. Jonathan is a native of the Niger Delta and a former governor of an oil-producing state. He is a member of the Ijaw ethnic group and a Christian. In April 2011, Jonathan was declared victor in the national presidential election, winning in both the Christian south and the Muslim north.

On several occasions since the restoration of civilian rule in 1999, Nigeria's military has carried out severe reprisals against civilian populations, including the destruction of entire communities. Nigeria's police are accused of routinely torturing criminal suspects and have the reputation of being highly corrupt and ineffective. Politicians, both federal and state, routinely

---

[2]   For a recent and concise review of stability in Nigeria, see *Nigeria: Assessing Risks to Stability* (Lewis, 2011).

[3]   University confraternities, which were initially similar to the elite fraternal social organizations common in the United States, devolved into violent criminal organizations after Nigeria's authoritarian ruler, General Ibrahim Beadamasi Babangida, decided in 1985 to provide them with weapons (Davis, 2009b, p. 114). Babangida sought to use these confraternities to counter opponents to his regime, especially the left-leaning student unions and prodemocracy activists present on many university campuses ("Nigeria: Cults of Violence," 2008). Nigerians started calling the confraternities "cults" in the 1980s because some of the organizations were secretive and practiced voodoo or tribal rituals (Asuni, 2009b, p. 8).

hire gangs of thugs to attack their opponents, steal ballot boxes, and intimidate voters. These gangs include university-based fraternitylike organizations, street gangs composed of unemployed youths, and cult-based groups. Gang members are often paid with government funds. These gangs have been accused of participating in a broad range of criminal activities, including extortion, assassination, rape, and drug trafficking. Even as the gangs and cults became more violent and destructive, politicians, security agencies, and military leaders continued to arm them and sought their support against other factions (Davis, 2009b, p. 132; "Nigeria: Cults . . . ," 2008). Indeed, it has been alleged that many of Nigeria's politicians are themselves members of these gangs and cults.

In the Niger Delta, poverty and the longstanding grievances of the local population against their federal and state governments and against international oil companies fuel the threat to the energy sector. The dominant view of the delta's inhabitants has been that the international oil companies act in the interest of the federal government, that oil production creates few local jobs, and that pollution from oil production has destroyed traditional sources of income such as fishing and agriculture (Asuni, 2009b, p. 6; Nossiter, 2010; Davis, 2009a, p. 5). Historically, the federal and state governments and international oil companies have absorbed the profits of oil operations, causing the inhabitants of the delta to feel that they reap little tangible benefit. Elements of the delta population are thus motivated both to express political grievances and to seek a livelihood through theft of oil and oil equipment and the kidnapping and ransom of oil workers.

Against this backdrop, groups that threaten the energy infrastructure have tended to find a hospitable local population. This in turn makes it very difficult for the government to ensure security in the region. The April 2011 electoral victory of President Goodluck Jonathan, with strong support from the population in the delta, his native region, could bring about reforms that would diminish resentment toward the central government.[4]

The Threat from Armed Groups

A variety of armed groups in the Niger Delta contribute to the chronic instability of the region and disrupt oil production.[5] The last comprehensive survey, conducted in 2007, identified 48 distinct groups comprising more than 25,000 members in the Delta State alone (Asuni, 2009b, p. 3). Most of these groups are criminally motivated, although one very active group, the Movement for the Emancipation of the Niger Delta (MEND), has also been motivated by resentment of the national government and of the international oil companies that have been perceived to be in league with it.

There have been attempts to form settlements and peace agreements with the armed groups; each attempt has met only temporary success. Even in the event that an armed group turns in its weapons as a part of a peace agreement, it can easily rearm.

---

[4] Jonathan did, however, make *Time*'s 100 Most Influential People list in 2012, with President Ellen Johnson Sirleaf of Liberia writing that he has "spearheaded the fight against corruption and turned Nigeria into an example of good governance" (Sirleaf, 2012).

[5] The core states of the Niger Delta—and the centers of violence—are Rivers, Bayelsa, and Delta. Officially, however, the Niger Delta also includes the states of Akwa Ibom, Cross River, Abia, Edo, Imo, and Ondo. See Jane's Terrorism Insurgency Centre (JTIC), 2009, p. 5.

Criminal Groups

In the 1990s, certain of the so-called confraternities morphed into criminal organizations that engaged in oil bunkering (Asuni, 2009b, p. 10; Davis, 2009a, pp. 114–115). Competition between these groups escalated as they struggled to gain control over this and other criminal activities (Wellington, 2007). As a result of this growing violence, many communities in the delta found themselves in peril. Finding that they could not rely on the police for protection, they formed vigilante groups to secure their neighborhoods from these criminal organizations. The vigilantes that emerged in the 1990s turned out to be little better than the groups they were formed to combat. After the vigilantes defeated the organizations that had encroached upon their community, it was not uncommon for the vigilantes themselves to assume control over the vanquished groups' illicit activities and to become involved in rivalries with other criminal organizations (Davis, 2009b, p. 16–121). In sum, there is a legacy of armed groups in the Niger Delta that have engaged in a violent competition for control over the region's illegal operations, oil bunkering in particular.

The Niger Delta Vigilantes (NDV) is one of the largest and most notorious of the criminal organizations operating in the Niger Delta. Its leader, Ateke Tom, is known for promoting and participating in extreme acts of violence against local civilians, as well as other criminal organizations. He has a long history of illegal bunkering for profit, and bunkering is one of NDV's principal criminal activities. NDV thus presents a serious continuing threat to energy security in Nigeria.

Politically Motivated Militants

There is also a sizable politically motivated organization that has posed a threat to oil production: MEND. This group evolved from a loose coalition of regional ethnic Ijaw armed groups in the 1990s to a unified organization in 2005. The arrest of Ijaw leader Mujahid Dokubu-Asari in September 2005 catalyzed gang leaders and political militants to pool their forces, unite under the name of MEND, and launch the first attack against the oil industry four months later, in January 2006 (Asuni, 2009b, pp. 16–17; Junger, 2007). MEND views the oil industry, especially the companies operating on shore, such as Shell, as being closely linked to and overly supportive of the government.

MEND has attempted to distinguish itself from the other armed groups in the Niger Delta by emphasizing a populist message that reflects the grievances of the local population. Until recently, this strategy had largely succeeded as MEND maintained a considerable degree of popular support. MEND's core demands have been (1) that the government release imprisoned militant leaders, (2) that the oil companies compensate the inhabitants of the delta for the damage to the environment, (3) that the central government grant the people a greater share of the oil profits, and (4) that the federal government invest in developing the infrastructure and economy of the region (JTIC, 2009, p. 34; Asuni, 2009b, p. 18).

The militants' good relationship with the communities in the Niger Delta and the MEND's decentralized structure have made it difficult for the Nigerian armed forces and police to defeat it. There have been a few attempts at reconciliation. In August 2009, the government struck a deal with a number of militant leaders to persuade their followers to lay down their weapons in return for amnesty, financial compensation, and retraining (Duffield, 2009; ICG, 2009, p. 1). Additional investment to improve living conditions in the delta was also promised. Over 15,000 militants found the government's offer enticing and turned in their weapons. The truce, however, was shaky. As one young militant said, "They, the government, they have every power. Let them do as they say. If they don't? Then, I will bust pipelines again. That is the truth." The ailing health of then–President Yar'Adua, however, delayed the continuation of peace talks between the government and the militants and sparked a resurgence of attacks (Edirin, 2010). Indeed, the frequent hospitalizations of Yar'Adua caused many such agreements and truces to be suspended.

Upon Yar'Adua's death, President Jonathan took office and rapidly gained the support of MEND and other militant groups because he, like the militants, is an ethnic Ijaw from the delta (BBC News, 2011). Nevertheless, two bombs detonated during the Independence Day celebrations in October 2010, and attacks on the energy infrastructure have continued (BBC News, 2011).

The recent election strengthens President Jonathan's negotiating position with MEND and might defuse local support for MEND's antigovernment agenda. These developments alone, however, are unlikely to bring a halt the militant actions of MEND's members. In recent years, MEND has drifted into illegal activities and blurred the line between supporting the aspirations of the local population and profiting from criminal activities.

Attacks on the Energy Industry and Onshore Infrastructure

MEND, NDV, and other groups have engaged in a wide range of operations against the energy infrastructure in the Niger Delta. The chief varieties are kidnappings, destructive attacks on infrastructure, and oil bunkering. A typical objective of an attack is to seize foreigners, usually employees of the international oil companies, who can be held hostage for ransom (Bergen Risk Solutions, 2007, p. 3).

The vast majority of the attacks occur onshore or in 65 km of Nigeria's coastline (Bergen Risk Solutions, 2007, p. 9; Giroux, 2008). On land, the oil pipelines are often exposed and unguarded; onshore terminals are also at risk because of their large, open oil and gas storage tanks and because they are located near villages and rivers where militants can hide (ICG, 2006a, p. 24; Tattersall, 2008).

Bunkering
Bunkering is a significant drain on Nigeria's energy sector. Some of the larger criminal organizations organize large-scale bunkering, which involves stealing large quantities of crude and using slow-moving barges to transport the oil out of the delta so that it can be sold abroad. The barges used to transport the stolen crude hold anywhere from 30,000 to 500,000 barrels of oil. The barges deliver their cargo to tankers, which then carry the oil to spot markets or refineries abroad (Asuni, 2009a, p. 5).

Since it is complicated to steal, transport, and sell large quantities of oil, the bunkerers are thought to rely on, at a minimum, the negligence and, often, the active collusion of the police, military, and local politicians (ICG, 2006a, p. 9).

In late 2004, the government directed the Nigerian Navy to step up its efforts to interdict the barges carrying stolen crude. The operation has met with some success. Large-scale bunkering declined, although few bunkerers have been apprehended (Davis, 2007, p. 12).

Attacks on the Offshore Infrastructure

There have been only a few attacks on offshore infrastructure. There are fewer offshore installations (less than ten) than onshore installations, and the logistics of mounting an attack are more challenging.

Both factors could change, however. A combination of technological breakthroughs that enable deep-water drilling and the discovery of rich offshore fields has led to a shift in the production of oil offshore. As militants develop more sophisticated capabilities, offshore facilities could be at risk as well. We have seen a preview of this. In June 2008, a party of MEND militants attacked Shell's Bonga floating production, storage, and offloading (FPSO) vessel (see Figure 3.1). At more than 300 m long, Bonga is one of the world's largest FPSOs. It sits 120 km offshore in the Gulf of Guinea and had been thought to be beyond the reach of insurgents (JTIC, 2009, p. 10). Even though MEND did not achieve its objective, which was to reach Bonga's control room, the attack caused panic in the oil markets, when Shell invoked force majeure and halted the Bonga platform's June and July 2008 production, which is normally 225,000 bpd (Tattersall, 2008; Daly, 2008).[6] Militant attacks on deep-water facilities have not yet increased since the Bonga strike, although it did demonstrate that such attacks are in the capabilities of at least one militant group.

The environmental impact of both the attacks on, and the work of, the oil and gas industry has been severe. Between 1986 and 1996, 2.5 million barrels of oil leaked into delta waterways, eliminating the fish stocks upon which the locals rely. The fresh water around the oil wells is too polluted to drink. Gas flaring has produced a blighting acid rain (Junger, 2007). Much of the oil pollution in the creeks is caused by bunkering (Figure 3.2).

Figure 3.1
**Side View of 300-Meter-Long Shell Bonga Floating
Production, Storage, and Offloading Vessel**

SOURCE: Shell. Used in accordance with Creative Commons License terms.
RAND *TR1144z4-3.1*

---

[6] *Force majeure* [greater force] is a legal clause inserted in contracts to absolve someone of responsibility if an unanticipated event beyond the control of the party prevents it from fulfilling its contractual obligations.

Figure 3.2
Aerial View Showing Oil Seepage from Bunkering Activities in the Niger Delta Region

SOURCE: Copyright 2010 Google; copyright 2010 GeoEye.
RAND TR1144z4-3.2

CHAPTER FOUR

Nigeria's Armed Forces

Nigeria's police and armed forces have not proven equal to securing the energy infrastructure. Most members of the Nigerian armed forces are undertrained and underequipped. Each of the three branches also suffers from varying levels of corruption and mismanagement. Moreover, in the Niger Delta, the task is daunting. Shell alone has more than 3,720 miles of oil and gas pipelines in the creeks, as well as 90 oil fields and 73 flow stations—a vast infrastructure to secure (Junger, 2007). This chapter presents a brief overview of current status of the Nigeria's military forces, as relevant to petroleum infrastructure protection.

Army

The Nigerian Army is 70,000 strong, by far the largest in Africa. At any given time, however, much of the army's equipment is nonoperational and operational readiness low.

Since 2006, Nigeria has attempted to instill greater democratic principles into the army in an effort to professionalize the force. Low morale is a particular problem. Soldiers frequently claim that they do not receive full payment for participating in peacekeeping missions. In addition, low salaries and inadequate provisions allocated to soldiers encourage corruption, which further undermines their reliability and effectiveness (JTIC, 2009, p. 44).

In the delta, the bulk of the army's attention has been focused on combating MEND. Success has been limited, and the army has been unable to prevent attacks on oil installations. Moreover, raids on communities suspected of harboring militants have deepened ill feeling between the army and the delta population, further complicating their efforts to secure the region's energy-producing infrastructure.

Nigeria also deploys troops to international peacekeeping missions in Africa. At the beginning of 2011, Nigerian peacekeepers were part of eight different missions, two of which included substantial deployments (Jane's, 2011).

Table 4.1 summarizes the Nigerian Army's equipment inventory. While the total numbers are substantial, the numbers actually operationally ready at any given time are much lower and difficult to determine with any precision. Major equipment, such as battle tanks and armored vehicles, has little value against the mobile criminal groups operating in the Niger Delta.

Air Force

With a strength of 9,500, the Nigerian Air Force is the largest air force in West Africa. It continues to suffer from readiness deficiencies, although this may change in response to recent

Table 4.1
Major Equipment of the Nigerian Army

Type	Weapon	Current Inventory
Armor	Main battle tank	276
	Light tank	157
	Reconnaissance	452
	Armored personnel carrier	484+
Artillery	Self-propelled howitzer	39
	Towed howitzer	112
	Multiple rocket launcher	25
Air-defense	Man-portable surface-to-air missile	148
	Self-propelled surface-to-air missile	16
	Antiaircraft gun	90+

SOURCE: International Institute for Strategic Studies (IISS), 2011.

increasing emphasis on training and maintenance (Jane's, 2011). It has focused on supporting the Nigerian Army by transporting troops and materiel. The air force's ability to provide close air support is limited because of shortfalls in training and the operational availability of suitable aircraft (Table 3.2). The service has not had a significant maritime role in protecting the offshore energy infrastructure. This may also be changing. In May 2011, the air force chief of staff, Air Marshall Mohammed Dikko Umar, announced that the Nigerian Air Force would like to revive and expand its maritime search-and-rescue capabilities (Jane's, 2012).

During the years of military rule, the Nigerian Air Force was implicated in a plot against the government, which led the military government to eviscerate it. With the return of civilian government in 1999, strengthening the air force became a priority, although progress has been slow. For example, in 2007, the service's air marshal informed the Nigerian legislature that all the nation's fighter jets were inoperable, leaving the force with only a few functioning rotary-wing craft.

The Nigerian Air Force can periodically marshal a small number of Russian-made Mi-17 and Mi-24 Hind attack helicopters, some AW139 VIP transport helicopters, and Super Puma troop transports. In January 2009, Air Marshal Petinrin announced impending delivery of 12 Chinese Chengdu F-7NI combat aircraft and three FT-7NI two-seat trainers, with the manufacturer providing air force pilots and engineering staff with familiarization training on the Chinese aircraft (Jane's, 2010b).

In December 2009, the air force received the first of two Italian-made ATR 42 MP maritime patrol aircraft ordered from Alenia. They are equipped with Selex Galileo's Airborne Tactical Observation and Surveillance system, which permits broad surveillance tracking of objects on the ocean's surface (Kington, 2009). This addition gave the air force a rudimentary capability to conduct surveillance over Nigeria's coastline and exclusive economic zone.

Table 4.2
Nigerian Air Force: Equipment in Service

	Type	Combat Capable (number)
Aircraft	Fighter	15
	Fighter ground attack	9
	Fighter ground attack/ISR	12
	Maritime patrol	2
	Transport	53
	Trainer	100
Helicopters	Attack	93
	Transport	4
	Trainer	N/A

SOURCE: IISS, 2011.

Navy

The Nigerian navy is also in a low state of operational readiness. The most serious problem is the lack of serviceable vessels. At any given time, most Nigerian naval vessels are not available for operation because of poor maintenance. The navy has managed, however, to increase its patrols in the Niger Delta, which seems to have deterred most large-scale bunkering.

The Nigerian government has made rebuilding the navy a priority and, in 2009, launched a program to expand and refurbish the fleet (Mazumdar, 2009). A stated goal of the navy is to strengthen local capacity to deal with oil theft and piracy.

In 2006, Nigeria, along with 25 other African countries, committed to developing a joint coast guard force that would have the right to pursue criminals and pirates into neighboring states' waters (Jane's, 2011). There are concerns, however, that the plans are too ambitious. As one observer has noted, Nigeria's needs would best be met by working to better maintain its existing brown-water fleet and improving training so that the navy can operate the equipment it has (Mazumdar, 2009). Currently, either the navy or the federal Maritime Police fulfill the coast guard role, with the latter being outside the Ministry of Defense. The navy's Special Boat Service operates in rivers and the littoral.

Table 4.3 summarizes the navy's equipment holdings, including its aviation and coast guard capabilities. As with the other services, the number of operationally ready craft is much smaller. An additional surface combatant will be soon added when the Nigerian navy finishes refurbishing a former U.S. Coast Guard high-endurance cutter. Patrol and coastal combatants include 15 *Defender*-class response boats from the United States, four Suncraft 17-m Manta Mk II ASD fast patrol craft, two Malaysian 38-m patrol craft, and two Israeli Shaldag MK-II fast petrol boats. In addition to these recent acquisitions, the navy has 14 Dutch-made K38 fast catamarans from TP Marine in service (not shown in Table 4.3), with six more on the way. For lack of adequate training, the catamarans have largely remained unused (Jane's, 2011). In the summer of 2008, the United States furnished and installed a coastal surveillance system, to be operated by the Nigerian Air Force, that uses radar sonar infrared to track vessels in Nigerian

Table 4.3
Nigerian Navy: Equipment in Service

	Type	Number
Surface Fleet	Principal surface combatants	1
	Patrol and coastal combatants	20
	Mine countermeasures	2
	Amphibious	1
	Logistics and support	5
Coast Gurad	Coastal patrol craft	39
	Patrol craft	9
	Hovercraft	5
Naval Aviation	Helicopter, antisubmarine	9
	Helicopter, multirole	5
	Helicopter, transport	3

SOURCE: IISS, 2011.

waters. As of this writing, there has been little indication that the information this surveillance system gathers has been utilized or that the country has shared the information with the United States, as Nigeria had agreed to do (Asuni, 2009a, p. 9).

The Nigerian Military Response in the Niger Delta

To counter violence and theft in the Niger delta, Nigeria operates a joint task force (JTF), comprising members of the army, navy, and air force, plus members of the police and state security offices. JTF units are often stationed immediately adjacent to major onshore facilities, such as petroleum storage and loading terminals. Mobile police units are sometimes stationed inside the perimeters of major facilities, and these federal police units routinely provide security to oil company employees as they travel in the country. The Nigerian Air Force has been able to provide very limited close air support to the Nigerian Army, primarily using helicopter gunships. Overall, the JTF is poorly trained and frequently overpowered by militias (Jane's, 2012).

The circumstances in the Niger Delta would challenge any military. Nigeria has been hard pressed to cope with assaults on the delta's oil-producing infrastructure. One reason is the complicity of Nigerian government and military officials in the activities of the militias and armed groups. Another reason is simply that the limited operational capacity of the Nigerian military to deal with these groups.

In spite of being underequipped and undertrained and having low morale, the Nigerian military has registered some limited successes. By expanding the number of patrols in the Niger Delta, the Special Boat Service and the Maritime Police seem to have deterred most of the large-scale bunkering (Davis, 2007, p. 12). The task force has also stepped up its actions to counter oil theft and has curtailed some of the most brazen oil bunkering activities. After MEND rejected President Yar'Adua's offer of amnesty, the JTF launched an offensive against

MEND in May 2009 that targeted militant camps and freed a number of hostages. MEND soon agreed to a ceasefire, and a large number of MEND members, including most of the senior commanders, formally laid down their arms (Lewis, 2011). The ceasefire continued until January 2010 but was frequently violated by second-tier commanders during the power vacuum in the Nigerian government associated with the illness of President Yar'Adua.

In sum, threats to the oil-producing and transporting infrastructure onshore are difficult to cope with. Improving the security of the oil-producing infrastructure onshore will hinge more on improving relations between the federal government and the delta's population, coupled with effective, incorrupt policing. As production steadily moves offshore, however, aviation forces can make a stronger contribution to securing the infrastructure.

CHAPTER FIVE

U.S. Air Force Roles in Promoting Energy Security

This concluding chapter examines the contributions that the U.S. Air Force could make to energy security in the Gulf of Guinea. Our emphasis is on Nigeria, for good reason: it produces the bulk of the region's energy, has the greatest potential for increasing production, and faces an active threat to its energy-producing infrastructure. Further, because of its large population, large area, and abundant natural resources, Nigeria will play a key, if not the dominant, role in future political, social, and economic development of West Africa.

Based on petroleum and natural gas production trends, the threat assessment, and current Nigerian military capabilities, our analysis suggests that the most productive approach for improving energy security would focus on building the Nigerian Air Force's ability to provide surveillance of the offshore energy infrastructure located in Nigeria's exclusive economic zone and to support a rapid incident response capability.

Our focus is on offshore protection because that is where nearly all new petroleum and natural gas production, both in Nigeria and in nearby nations, is taking place. Additionally, attackers of offshore installations must travel on the water's surface, which means they are exposed. With the aid of a cueing system, an aircraft has a good chance of picking up a target and then tracking it. Moreover, offshore facilities require a substantial capital investment and individually produce much more than does a typical onshore facility. Cost-benefit considerations therefore justify a sizable investment in the security of these facilities. In contrast, onshore oil installations and their environs are covered by a dense canopy of heavy foliage, enabling attackers to operate clandestinely; surveillance and tracking from the air is marginally effective at best. Additionally, the onshore oil infrastructure is much more fragmented, consisting of many modest-size facilities spread out over a broad area. The output of each individual production facility is modest compared to those of the large offshore facilities, making it harder to justify substantial investment in an expensive security system, even if it could work operationally.

While attacks on the offshore infrastructure have been relatively limited thus far, the current situation may not last. As production continues to shift offshore, we can expect militants to turn their attention to these lucrative targets.

The driving consideration promoting the utility of air-based assets is that the offshore infrastructure is widely dispersed, spread over some 64,000 km^2. This is far too great an area to be patrolled by ships; airborne surveillance is thus the only practical option for Nigeria if it is to monitor emerging incidents or respond promptly if one takes place.

At present, there is no effective deterrent to an offshore attack. Here, the U.S. Air Force can make an important contribution by partnering with the Nigerian Air Force to build the latter's capabilities. Our research does not support a recommendation that has such a partnership between the two air forces focusing on protection of the onshore assets. The heavy foliage canopy makes surveillance and tracking from the air prohibitively difficult.

While there is a clear opportunity to build capabilities that can improve energy security, partnering with Nigeria poses serious challenges that must be addressed if the U.S. Air Force is to make a meaningful contribution.

Challenges to Partnering with Nigeria

Nigeria's Willingness to Partner

Nigeria has been reluctant to have foreign military present in the country. It publicly opposed U.S. plans to locate AFRICOM headquarters on the continent out of fear that it would serve the interests of the United States at the expense of Nigeria's. Indeed, in its public statements, Nigerian leaders have been very sensitive to any criticism that their policies would promote U.S. or other foreign interests. An example of local opposition to outside military intervention was the backlash in the Niger Delta to British Prime Minister Gordon Brown's 2008 proposal to supply military support to the Nigerian armed forces (Asuni, 2009a, p. 8).[1]

On the other hand, the Nigerian military recognizes its need for assistance in training its forces and for modern military equipment along with the ability to sustain it. It has partnered with the United States in a number of capacity-building activities. It has been a robust participant in the U.S.-sponsored African Contingency Operations Training and Assistance program, sending more than 10,000 personnel to be trained in peacekeeping skills. It has steadily expanded its participation in the International Military Education and Training program since its return to democratic rule in 1999. Other cooperative security activities with United States have included

- air forces
  - a U.S. Air Force team that deployed in 2009 to assist the Nigerian Air Force with C-130 maintenance
  - air domain and safety initiatives, including a 2010 disaster-response exercise hosted in Indianapolis
  - plans for pilot training at Vance Air Force Base and for maintenance training at Shepherd Air Force Base
- maritime
  - Nigerian Navy participation in the ongoing African Partnership Station program sponsored by the U.S. Navy[2]
  - installation, with U.S. assistance, of a system of radars and automated identification system receivers known as the Regional Maritime Awareness Capability, designed to allow Nigeria and São Tome and Principe to monitor ship traffic in the Gulf of Guinea
- other
  - Nigerian participation in the U.S. Department of State–led Trans-Sahara Counter-Terrorism Partnership program.

---

[1] Asuni suggests that the furor over Brown's offer resulted from the efforts of some Ijaw leaders to retain control over the militants.

[2] This program promotes seamanship, search and rescue, and maritime domain awareness skills among African navies and encourages regional maritime cooperation.

A key characteristic these programs have in common is that they have a relatively light in-country footprint. This would be important in launching any new initiative. Working with the U.S. military is controversial with large parts of Nigerian society (indeed in most parts of Africa). Working with the Nigerian Air Force mitigates problem because cooperation would take place on air bases, which are largely isolated from population centers.

The State of Governance in Nigeria

As discussed in Chapter Six, the Nigerian government has a long record of governance problems. Of the World Bank's six governance indicators, Nigeria ranks in the lowest 10 percentile on political stability and government effectiveness. And it ranks well below the 25th percentile on control of corruption and the application of the rule of law (Kaufmann, Kraay, and Mastruzzi, 2010). Most seriously, human rights continue to be consistently violated in Nigeria.[3]

Consequently, in shaping a capacity-building program with Nigeria, two other factors are important. Care must be taken to ensure

- that our presence is not perceived as our "taking sides" in internal divisions in Nigeria
- that partnering with the Nigerian Air Force does not build a capacity likely to be used against the population.

The importance of these two factors was highlighted during our discussions with representatives of several international oil companies that have significant onshore and offshore investments and operations in Nigeria.[4] These oil companies have seen violence and theft disrupt their current operations in the delta, particularly their onshore operations. Their representatives acknowledged that this has not only constrained output but has been a deterrent to the investments necessary to expand hydrocarbon production in Nigeria. Yet they were cautious about, and in one case strongly opposed to, any action the U.S. government might take that could disrupt the status quo or that could be viewed as "taking sides" or increasing repression in the Niger Delta.[5]

Nigeria's human rights record raises a crucial issue for any U.S. efforts to build military capabilities in Nigeria: Can Nigeria be trusted not to use these additional capabilities to suppress dissent and otherwise exert military force on its civilian population?

---

[3] According to U.S. Department of State, 2010:

> Human rights problems during the year included the abridgement of citizens' right to change their government; politically motivated and extrajudicial killings by security forces, including summary executions; vigilante killings; abductions by militant groups; torture, rape, and other cruel, inhuman or degrading treatment of prisoners, detainees, and criminal suspects; harsh and life-threatening prison and detention center conditions; arbitrary arrest and prolonged pretrial detention; denial of fair public trial; executive influence on the judiciary and judicial corruption; infringement of privacy rights; restrictions on freedom of speech, press, assembly, religion, and movement; official corruption and impunity; domestic violence and discrimination against women; the killing of children suspected of witchcraft; female genital mutilation . . . ; child abuse and child sexual exploitation; societal violence; ethnic, regional, and religious discrimination; trafficking in persons for the purpose of prostitution and forced labor; discrimination against persons with disabilities; discrimination based on sexual orientation and gender identity; and child labor.

[4] The oil company representatives that we spoke with typically held positions in their companies' global security or regional affairs divisions.

[5] Appendix B further elaborations on the perspectives of the relevant international oil companies.

Nigeria's Current Military Capabilities

Any partnership to build Nigerian Air Force capabilities will, of necessity, have to begin modestly. The air force has significant shortfalls in training its personnel and maintaining its equipment. Capability development will have to begin with the basics and ensure that training and maintenance procedures are in place so that the newly acquired capabilities endure after the U.S. Air Force team is finished.

The obstacles to partnering with the Nigerian Air Force are challenging but by no means insurmountable. The Nigerian military recognizes its need for assistance in training its forces and for modern military equipment. The Nigerian federal government, moreover, depends on the earnings generated by the export of oil for some 80 percent of its revenue (the size of the oil-derived share fluctuates with the rise and fall of the price of oil). This provides a strong incentive to improve its ability to secure the oil-producing infrastructure.

A Framework for Partnering with Nigeria

Our framework for partnering with Nigeria drew on recent RAND research on best practices to increase international security cooperation and assure operational practicality (Moroney et al., 2010). These best practices consist of a five-step framework, which has been tailored to cooperation with Nigeria through interviews with officers at AFRICOM headquarters, the 17th Air Force, and the country team in Nigeria. This framework, as it could apply to building partner capacity with Nigeria (and with minor modification, other nations in the Gulf of Guinea), is outlined below.

First, understand the objectives and purposes of the program under construction. At this stage, it is critical to ensure that the objectives of any security cooperation plan are linked to higher-level guidance. In the present case, securing diverse sources of energy imports is a stated objective in the President's *National Security Strategy* and in the *Quadrennial Defense Review Report* (White House, 2010; DoD, 2010). A clear objective, tied to a security cooperation purpose, guides the choice of the potential partner. A security cooperation plan with Nigeria or another country in the Gulf of Guinea should therefore be formulated in the context of long-term objectives. Beginning with modest initiatives is appropriate and should form the foundation for addressing broader problems.

Second, identify the appropriate security cooperation program based on the purpose and objectives as defined. The security cooperation purpose is derived from the objective, which in turn is derived from the various strategic guidance documents that might drive the need for planning.

Third, select appropriate potential partner nations. Purpose-specific programs tend to assume a partner; this study focuses on Nigeria because our purpose was to examine actions the Air Force could take to promote energy security and the continued growth of the hydrocarbon production sector in the Gulf of Guinea, of which Nigeria is by far the greatest contributor. However, many programs are broad enough to be applied to a variety of partners, so there could well be similar programs with other countries in the region.

Fourth, prioritize a list of potential partners. This requires a two-part process that differentiates the relative merits of each. First, the security cooperation planner organizes countries into employment partners, development partners, and posture partners. This highlights the operational and technical merits. Part two, a "second look" prioritization, examines the natures of the potential partners (e.g., quality of governance, internal stability, and ability to absorb assistance). This, together with the nature of the relationship the United States has with the potential partners, provides the framework for deciding which potential partners are suitable to work with. The Nigeria of the 1990s, when it was ruled by a military dictatorship, would almost certainly not have been deemed a suitable partner. Although corruption is still a concern, governance has improved, and Nigeria has recently conducted an election deemed legitimate by international observers.

The fifth and final step is to select the appropriate security cooperation activities. These depend on the country's own capacity to absorb assistance. When such a capability is low but emerging, potential activities would include needs and capabilities assessments, training, conferences and workshops, and other low-level programs. When a country is developing, more advanced activities, such as education programs, joint exercises, and equipment training, would be appropriate. Finally, an advanced country would benefit from personnel exchanges and research, development, test, and evaluation funds.

In this context, therefore, recommendations follow for initiating a partnering program with Nigeria's air force that begins with less challenging security cooperation activities. Successful completion of these activities could form the foundation for midlevel activities. The initial steps are modest taken by themselves but are crucial to laying the foundation for a broader, long-term partnership.

A Modest Beginning for Building Nigerian Capacity

Considering the three challenges of military partnering with Nigeria, especially Nigeria's history of human rights violations, we suggest considering a partnership between the U.S. and Nigerian air forces that would *initially* focus on developing capabilities that are more benign but that nonetheless lay the groundwork for capabilities that contribute directly to energy infrastructure protection. Key examples are search and rescue, medical evacuation, and exclusive economic zone enforcement. They are low visibility and noncontroversial. While the first two examples are humanitarian missions, they share much of the same basic skill set as for aerial surveillance, RTT, and command, control, and communications. These activities could serve as a noncontroversial entry point for partnering with the Nigerian Air Force and as a vehicle for partner capacity building that could build the foundation for a capability to respond to and deter attacks on hydrocarbon-producing infrastructure.

Search and Rescue
Responding to an incident involving the offshore infrastructure has elements in common with a maritime search-and-rescue operation. The role of airborne surveillance is broadly analogous: On warning, fly promptly to the location of the incident and identify a vessel. The key difference is that the vessel in question would be in distress rather than under or perpetrating an attack. Directing and coordinating a search requires command and control facilities, which could serve as the foundation for capabilities required for operations to protect the offshore energy-producing infrastructure.

Medical Evacuation

Successful aeromedical evacuation operations require some of the same capabilities as RTT: On alert, fly promptly via helicopter to austere locations. A program focusing on this could be introduced as part of existing assistance programs focused on peacekeeping, such as Africa Contingency Operations Training and Assistance. Nigeria personnel form the core of a number of African peacekeeping deployments, and improving the country's vertical lift medical evacuation capacity would also support the peacekeeping deployments of Nigerian military units.

Exclusive Economic Zone Enforcement

Hydrocarbon production is not Nigeria's only offshore interest. Both large-scale and traditional fishing operations exploit the valuable fisheries in the Gulf of Guinea. Maritime surveillance and reconnaissance can help Nigeria and other Gulf of Guinea countries build a picture of who is fishing in controlled waters to serve as a basis for enforcement. Exclusive economic zone enforcement is on the current list of missions for the Nigerian Air Force's new ATR-42 aircraft (Vogelaar, 2010). Nigeria could welcome U.S. Air Force assistance in improving airborne patrol tactics and concepts of operation for exclusive economic zone enforcement, which could form the foundation for aerial surveillance of the energy-producing infrastructure. The Regional Maritime Awareness Capability, described earlier, aims to provide a maritime domain picture to countries in the region using Automated Identification System receivers and radar. Surveillance aircraft can be used to investigate anomalies revealed by that fused operating picture. The operational experience gained readily translates into a capacity to respond to incidents on offshore oil-producing installations.

Building the Nigerian Air Force's Capacity for Energy Security

If the challenges to U.S. military cooperation with Nigeria can be addressed, a partnership between the two air forces could focus on offshore infrastructure protection. After discussing options for offshore infrastructure protection with officers at AFRICOM headquarters, the 17th Air Force, and the country team in Nigeria, we identified potential areas for U.S. assistance that intersected with important limitations of Nigerian capability. Three specific capabilities could address this problem:

- airborne surveillance
- RTT
- command, control, and communications.

Airborne Surveillance

The military experts and industry representatives we interviewed strongly acknowledged the value of airborne surveillance of the offshore environment. The U.S. Air Force has a strong capability in this area and, in recent years, has gained experience in collecting information on nontraditional threats.

Airborne surveillance addresses two of the key shortcomings in Nigeria's ability to combat infrastructure attacks: awareness of an attack and the ability to locate and track perpetrators. Hydrocarbon production continues to move to large offshore facilities, where aviation forces can operate unhindered by the heavy foliage canopy that obscures their view on land. Moreover, airborne surveillance, guided by timely intelligence of an impending attack, might detect and monitor threats before an incident occurs.

Nigeria's naval forces cannot fulfill this surveillance mission. The distances are too great to respond in a timely manner to an incident anywhere across the offshore energy infrastructure. An airborne surveillance platform, on the other hand, can move rapidly to the scene of an attack and, if necessary, search a broad area. This allows surveillance of far more of the infrastructure than patrol ships can offer, and the danger to an attacker of being identified and tracked is in itself a deterrent to attack.

Surveillance on this scale is relatively benign and has low-visibility and is thus unlikely to stir sensitivities among the population. Further, Nigeria has demonstrated an interest in improving its offshore airborne surveillance. The Nigerian Air Force has purchased two Italian-built ATR-42 maritime patrol aircraft. This provides a modest foundation for developing tactics and concepts of operation for a rudimentary response capability.

In summary, an initiative to build a Nigerian airborne surveillance capability would call on a core U.S. Air Force competency and would fill an important gap in Nigeria's ability to respond to tactical threats to the security of its energy infrastructure.

Rapid Tactical Transport

An effective deterrent to attacks on the offshore infrastructure would include the threat of being interdicted after airborne surveillance has identified and established a track on the attackers. This engagement is best effected by helicopter-mobile troops, although maritime forces have a complementary role to play. The air-mobile troops need not be numerous but should be an elite force with special operations forces–like training and should maintain a high level of readiness. This capability can be employed in response to offshore incidents. Offshore responses could include deploying to major offshore facilities that are equipped with helipads or deploying to intercept attackers as they reach shore.

The near-term capability could be rudimentary, based on a small fleet of transport helicopters that are relatively easy to maintain. In fact, whatever the Nigerian military's current or prospective difficulties in maintaining helicopters, the private energy sector makes extensive use of helicopters for transportation, with local contractors providing maintenance. Further, the Nigerian Civil Aviation Authority has recently moved to open a helicopter school at a Nigerian Air Force base (Areguamen, 2010). Even helicopters that fly only in the daytime and that must find suitable open terrain to set down troops will constrain attackers' options and can allow Nigeria's maritime forces to conduct a complementary intercept. The troops themselves require only rudimentary training to deploy from helicopters—the U.S. Army's basic air assault qualification course lasts for just ten days. A U.S. Southern Command foreign internal defense team could train the Nigerian assault force in other combat skills.

In Nigeria, as in most developing nations, rotary wing transport is an air force responsibility. On the U.S. side, either the Army or the Air Force could take a lead role in building this capability in Nigeria.

Command, Control, and Communications

Command, control, and communications are necessary to enable the other two areas. Airborne surveillance aircraft must be alerted, told to launch, and then directed appropriately. Rapid-response forces must be mustered and then directed according to real-time information from the surveillance aircraft.

Basic C3 for incident response is an appropriate, nonkinetic capability to develop among partners in the Gulf of Guinea. Staff at AFRICOM headquarters acknowledged that it would be best to design a situation command center like the one implied here from scratch and introduce it incrementally. The first step could be to establish a command center with a rudimentary communications network based on commercial systems. As procedures are developed, exercised, and refined, dedicated communication systems could be introduced.

Feasibility Review

Appendix A presents the results of an analysis of whether the performance necessary to carry out these missions is in the bounds of reasonable operational capacity. The analysis shows that a Nigerian pilot should be able to attain the skills necessary to operate in the timelines necessary to respond to an offshore incident. The key capability the Nigerian Air Force would have to develop would be maintaining two or three surveillance aircraft at a relatively high state of alert. With timely alert and launch, militants attacking an offshore facility could be intercepted and a track established. The rapid tactical response team would likewise need to be at a high state of readiness to launch promptly on notice of an incident.

An Attractive Alternative: Ghana

There are, however, other energy producers in the region who are better governed and have been more willing to work with the United States and who could benefit from the capabilities discussed here. If cooperation with Nigeria on energy security is not feasible in the near term, an alternative would be to work first with Ghana, a country that has good relations with the United States and that is relatively well-governed. As discussed in Chapter Two, substantial oil production from Ghana's offshore Jubilee field began in late 2011, with favorable prospects for continued growth in offshore production in the Jubilee field and elsewhere in Ghana's waters.

Ghana is one of the region's more stable governments. It has exhibited peaceful, democratic transitions of authority. It receives a "fully free" rating from Freedom House, a measure of political rights and civil liberties that only 20 percent of African nations share.

Ghana's small but reasonably capable armed forces are regarded as among West Africa's most professional (Jane's, 2009). The military is a reliable contributor to international peacekeeping efforts, and the U.S. military has a strong existing relationship with the Ghanaian armed forces. Ghana participates with the U.S. Navy in the Africa Partnership Station program and has worked with the United States through the African Contingency Operations Training and Assistance program since 2002. The Ghanaian Air Force recently purchased U.S. C-27J Spartan transport aircraft, showing both an interest in improving its air capacity and in doing so with a U.S.-compatible kit.

Its Air Force could likely benefit from further investment; it has capability gaps in the areas reviewed here. It has no dedicated surveillance aircraft. It does have a few transport helicopters, including some that it has successfully deployed in peacekeeping operations, a promising sign for its ability to maintain a RTT capability. As the offshore fields are developed, the government will have an incentive to develop the capacity to secure them. Assuming both governments agree, this appears to be a good mission for partnering with the U.S. military.

The U.S. Air Force, for example, could work with the Ghanaian Air Force to build an incident response capability in anticipation of the development of the offshore oil fields. As opportunities present themselves, the U.S. Air Force could extend the experience gained through working with Ghana to Nigeria and other countries in the region.

As in the case of Nigeria, the U.S. Air Force could begin by working with Ghana to build airborne surveillance and RTT capabilities for search and rescue. This would provide the foundation for developing an effective response to future threats to Ghana's planned offshore energy infrastructure.

Conclusion

In sum, the Gulf of Guinea has the potential to sustain and, indeed, expand its important role as an energy exporter. The U.S. Air Force can play an important role in building national capabilities to protect the growing offshore energy infrastructure. Considering current and forthcoming oil and natural gas production and the security threat, Nigeria is an obvious candidate for a military partnership directed at building local capabilities for protecting the energy supply chain. But Nigeria's dismal record of human rights violations suggests a cautious approach. Rather than move directly on building capabilities directed at protection of offshore energy assets, we suggest considering a phased approach in which the first step would be oriented toward maritime search and rescue, medical evacuation, and enforcement of Nigeria's exclusive economic zone. When and if the Nigerian government, including its military, eschews the use of military force against civilians, it may be appropriate for the U.S. Air Force to partner with the Nigerian Air Force to build capabilities in airborne surveillance, RTT, and C3. Whether Nigeria's new president is willing and able to make progress in this area remains uncertain.

Meanwhile, the Ghana Air Force presents an attractive opportunity for a partnership directed at building capacity to protect the nation's emerging offshore hydrocarbon industry.

A program of partnering would have to begin with very basic capabilities because of the limited capabilities of the local air forces and the shortcomings of their governments. That said, there are precedents whose successes can be drawn on to develop a workable program, and the potential payoff is substantial.

Analysis of Potential Aerial Operations

This appendix documents an analysis of the operational challenges the Nigerian Air Force would have to overcome to add significantly to the deterrence of attacks on the offshore energy-producing infrastructure. The operational analysis is based on the alert-response-search algorithm typical of maritime (coastal) search-and-rescue operations. The analysis indicates that a fairly modest incident response capability would give Nigeria the capacity to respond to incidents in the offshore area containing Nigeria's oil-producing infrastructure.

The analysis also provides information for setting target performance standards that would help the Nigerian Air Force, with capacity-building assistance from the U.S. Air Force, achieve this capability. The service has no such capability at present, and achieving the capability would, of necessity, be a gradual process. That process could start, for example, with a rudimentary search-and-rescue capability, which could be the foundation of an alert-response-tracking capability that would allow a prompt incident response. At each step of the way, the performance parameters that the Nigerian Air Force achieves can be plugged into an alert-response-search algorithm, such as the one we used in this analysis, to get a measure of the progress the service is making.

Analytic Framework

The analysis models a basic response to an attack without prior warning. For this type of incident, the surveillance aircraft would launch on notice of the incident, fly to the site to acquire and to establish a track on the attackers, and track them as they return to shore. Guided by the airborne surveillance aircraft, the RTT unit would interdict the attackers as they reach the shore. We constructed time lines to determine the number of bases and aircraft necessary to ensure a timely, credible response to an attack on any of 24 major Nigerian offshore facilities, which are positioned from 7 to 71 nmi out to sea.[1]

We did not attempt to model the performance of aerial assets that had specific cues for the time and location of the attack. However, the same assets might provide a capability to prevent a successful infrastructure attack by tracking and intercepting the perpetrators and/or by landing a tactical response unit on the target platform. Overall, developing a reactive (i.e., no prior warning) posture opens the possibility of responding to any attack, with, at the mini-

---

[1] We believe we have captured most, if not all, major offshore facilities and have at least covered each of the major offshore oil and gas fields. The facilities in question are a mix of FPSOs and terminals. The following analysis holds them of equal value, although some are more vital than others in practice. We established true latitudes and longitudes for 21 of the 24 and estimated the locations of the remaining three using a map of oil mining leases.

mum, a reasonable capability to intercept and capture (or kill) the perpetrators of the attack. This would be a strong deterrent.[2]

Key Assumptions

The model incorporates the following assumptions:

- The capabilities of the surveillance aircraft are equivalent to the ATR-42 and of the response aircraft are equivalent to the AS332 Super Puma helicopter. Both are aircraft currently in the Nigerian Air Force's inventory.
- Small-boats are detected with the naked eye from an altitude of 3,000 feet. If the target (hereafter referred to as the *red boat)* is in a sweep width of 3 nmi, a successful detection and identification is made.[3]
- The red boat's speed is 25 kts, and its bearing is ±22.5 degrees from the attacked facility to the shore.
- A search is considered successful if the red boat has no more than a 10-percent chance of avoiding detection before reaching shore.

Airborne Surveillance

We used an Excel-based model to analyze the potential benefits of an airborne surveillance capability. The results demonstrated the value of a fast response and thus of effective alerts and C3 procedures. Mission success depended on the aircraft establishing a search cordon that would ensure that the red boat would pass within visual range. The sooner the aircraft could initiate its search, the more effective its cordon. The key determinants of the time it takes the aircraft to arrive on the scene were speed of response from the attack to the aircraft launch and the distance between the air base and the attacked facility.

Results

Two cases were analyzed, one in which the aircraft received a launch order as soon as the attack occurred, the other with the aircraft receiving the order 10 minutes later. In both cases, the red attack lasted for 30 minutes, and the aircraft launched within 30 minutes of receiving word.[4]

---

[2]   This obviously would not apply if the militants engaged in suicide attacks, but they have not shown this proclivity.

[3]   The detection performance assumptions are intentionally conservative. As a point of reference, when visibility is limited to 5 nmi and when the target is a *stationary* 25-foot-long boat, the U.S. Navy's guide on search-and-rescue tactics recommends an unaided visual sweep width of 2.5 nmi (U.S. Department of the Navy, 1997). While poor visibility is common (though not omnipresent) in the Gulf of Guinea, the wake of a fast-moving boat could be detected at significantly greater range.

    We defaulted to naked-eye detection for two reasons. Given the small radar cross section of the target craft, clutter from Nigeria's large inshore fishing fleet, and the sea states involved, radar is not reliable for missions against small boats. The unaided eye offers a wider field of view than do electro-optical and infrared alternatives.

    Nighttime and bad weather will challenge this concept of operations.

[4]   The U.S. Coast Guard's objective performance standard for a search-and-rescue operation is 30 minutes (U.S. Coast Guard, 2009).

In the first case, an aircraft using an existing air base at Port Harcourt could cover 80 percent of the facilities.[5] In the second, an aircraft flying from Port Harcourt could cover only 45 percent of the major offshore facilities. Adding an second base helps. Locating the second at Warri, a sizable city with an airport and closer to the northerly offshore facilities, could increase coverage to 66 percent of the installations. With two entirely new bases sited at optimum locations, aircraft could cover over 90 percent of the offshore installations.

This analysis yields two insights. First, the Nigerian Air Force could cover a significant number of offshore facilities effectively simply using an existing base. Second, response speed offers a high payoff. A relatively brief delay in alert times sharply increases the resources required to achieve coverage.

Rapid Tactical Transport

The airborne surveillance capability in this analysis is coupled with an airborne RTT capability. The RTT aircraft's objective is to interdict the attackers' boat at landfall. We considered one helicopter carrying ten personnel, which should be able to achieve a successful tactical deployment at the shore point.

Results

As with airborne surveillance, we examined RTT performance with no delay in alert from the start of the attack and with a delay of 10 minutes. In both instances, the time the aircraft requires from alert to launch is set at the U.S. Coast Guard standard for response to a search-and-rescue alert, 30 minutes. Again, a comparatively small improvement in response time has a high payoff.

If there were no delay between attack and an alert message to the RTT, a helicopter launched from Port Harcourt could intercept the red boat before or as it reached the nearest landfall after returning from 70 percent of the facilities. When Warri is added to Port Harcourt, 23 of the 24 facilities could be covered.

In the second case, the red boat departs the facility 10 minutes before the aircraft launches. A Nigerian RTT aircraft based at Port Harcourt could successfully interdict attackers for 62 percent of the offshore facilities. Adding a second helicopter base at Warri would provide coverage of 75 percent of the facilities.

Command, Control, and Communications

Airborne surveillance and rapid tactical response require at least a rudimentary C3 capability. The parametric analysis above shows the payoff of a C3 system that can promptly alert the surveillance aircraft and rapid response troops.

Required Command, Control, and Communications

The requirement for timely response by both the surveillance aircraft and RTT aircraft establishes the following baseline C3 requirements:

---

[5] Port Harcourt is the only known Nigerian Air Force base in the delta.

- *The attacked facility must be able to communicate an incident alert to a command center.*[6] This analysis placed the burden for alert on the attacked party. It is a reasonable expectation: Manned oil facilities can communicate with the shore. Unmanned facilities can be alarmed, but are not targets for attackers seeking to steal or hold personnel for ransom. Nigerian military personnel at a command center need not be in direct contact with the offshore facility; for example, oil company personnel involved can send notice of the attack to their shore facilities, which can then use onshore infrastructure to pass the information to the command center.

- *The command center must have the ability and authority to launch the surveillance and the RTT response.* If the command center is colocated with the only operating location, communication is not a problem. For multiple operating bases, local communications infrastructure should be adequate for one location to dispatch a launch order to another promptly. The operational challenge is to assemble enough information about the attack to formulate the appropriate response. A key piece of information is where the attack took place. This will indicate which surveillance and RTT bases are closest (likely the same location) and thus which base or bases should respond with launching aircraft. The command center must monitor the status of the aircraft under its control and the nature of the attack.

- *Both the surveillance and RTT aircraft must be able to maintain real-time communication with the command center and with each other.* When the surveillance aircraft has acquired the attackers' boat, it will have to continuously communicate its location and expected landfall to the RTT helicopter. Both aircraft will need the ability to update the command center on the evolving situation from beyond line of sight. The C3 apparatus could also allow coordination with other forces. For example, maritime forces would strengthen an interdiction operation by adding the capability to interdict the attackers while still on the water.

Command, Control, and Communications Benefits

Aside from the requirement for at least a basic C3 capability to have an effective offshore incident response, enhanced C3 performance offers other benefits.

Efficient and timely C3 can increase response times. As shown in both the surveillance and RTT results, faster responses mean that the response force can deliver better performance with limited resources.

Preattack warning and shorter warning-to-launch times could also improve response performance.[7] Preattack warning could be increased by establishing exclusion zones around facilities, although local fishermen have largely ignored such exclusion zones in the past.[8] An aggressive alert posture might also improve warning-to-launch times, but our assumption in this area is already generous: Thirty minutes is the U.S. Coast Guard's objective time for search-and-rescue operations (U.S. Coast Guard, 2009). C3 improvements seem more promising.

---

[6] This discussion assumes a single command center. Some central authority is clearly necessary. If areas of responsibility were clearly established, however, multiple centers could be used.

[7] It would also be possible to improve response time by increasing aircraft speed beyond that of Nigeria's ATR-42.

[8] Conversations with representatives of American oil companies active in Nigeria.

A second benefit could be realized if the C3 capability were good enough to coordinate surveillance operations with multiple aircraft. The airborne surveillance analysis focused on an initial, rudimentary operation of one aircraft tracking for one boat. Having more than one aircraft available to pursue a single boat would greatly improve operational performance.[9]

Providing Capabilities

Our parametric analysis indicates that there are opportunities to enhance Nigerian military capability to deal with some of the threats to hydrocarbon operations. The airborne surveillance, RTT, and C3 capabilities described above could help provide Nigeria a strong deterrent response to the threat to key offshore facilities.

Airborne Surveillance

The U.S. Air Force has the opportunity in this area to begin with a capability Nigeria already has. The two ATR-42 maritime patrol aircraft are a good foundation that can be built on. The U.S. Air Force's initial objectives could be to work with the Nigerian Air Force to develop concepts of operation for search and rescue targeted on small boats. The mission shares many of the operational characteristics of the incidence response discussed above.

Rapid Tactical Transport

Recommendations in this area mirror those for airborne surveillance. Here, too, Nigeria already possesses a platform adequate for the RTT mission: the AS332 Super Puma helicopters recently ordered from France. They also have a collection of Soviet-era helicopters, although many are in bad repair. The U.S. Air Force could focus on tactics and concepts of operation, perhaps leveraging the renewed helicopter training effort at Enugu Air Base.

There is an advantage to adding platforms over time. The parametric capability analysis showed the utility of multiple operating locations to cover all offshore facilities. Further, the analysis examined a single red boat and a single RTT aircraft. While this is already a deterrent, the ability to handle additional boats would be desirable.

Command, Control, and Communications

Oil companies can already contact shore from their facilities, and the U.S. Air Force can build on this by encouraging the Nigerian military and the international oil companies to establish reliable ways to get alert messages to the incident response facility.

The C3 capability can also build on an existing U.S.-sponsored initiative, the Regional Maritime Awareness Capability. That initiative's goal is to establish a cooperative program with São Tome and Principe and Nigeria to monitor surface traffic in the Gulf of Guinea. A fused common operating picture, enabled by radar and Automatic Identification System transponders, is provided to several operations centers. The concept envisions tying in airborne sensors to investigate anomalies that it might detect, implying a planned or existing architecture for command center–to–aircraft communication that could be applied to the case at hand (Kasmierski, 2010).

---

[9] In particular, a broader swath of ocean could be searched, to cover cases where the fleeing red boat takes evasive maneuvers such as approaching the shore on an indirect route.

Perspectives of American Oil Companies

We met with representatives of several American oil companies that have significant operations in Nigeria both onshore and offshore. The representatives typically held positions in the companies' global security or regional affairs divisions.

Violence and theft have disrupt these companies' current operations in the delta, particularly onshore. The representatives acknowledged that this has not only constrained output but has deterred future investment in the region. Yet our interlocutors were cautious about, and in one case strongly opposed to, action that could disrupt the status quo.[1] Their security strategy, broadly speaking, has been to manage as best they could by building physical protective barriers around key installations and accepting the security that the Nigerian Mobile Police, a branch of the Nigerian federal police force, and the Nigerian military units assigned to protect the petroleum infrastructure provide. At the same time, they are building relationships with local governments and are taking steps to promote economic development in the delta. Since many locals regard the military as, at best, unwelcome and, at worst, a hostile presence, these American oil companies have adopted the strategy of avoiding close alignment with the military. Being too closely associated with the military, they fear, might increase the motivation for attacks on their infrastructure.

The net effect is that that these oil companies "tolerate" and work around the current burden on operations. Most discouraged U.S. efforts that would stimulate the Nigerian military to take more assertive action to gain central government authority in the delta. They feared that such action might drive up the overall level of violence to include violence against American oil companies. One representative did acknowledge that the Nigerian Navy's operations to intercept large barges that were transporting bunkered oil had significantly reduced high-end bunkering operations.

Offshore operations are another matter. The oil company representatives had mixed responses to the prospect of the Nigerian Armed Forces upgrading their capabilities for action offshore. When we asked about the benefits of "surveillance"—provided either commercially or via the U.S. government—their overall response was positive. The more situational aware-

---

[1] Oil company representatives and U.S. government officials indicated that recent Nigerian legislation could pose a bigger threat to energy investment than the security situation. The Petroleum Industry Bill and the Nigerian Oil and Gas Industry Development Bill (known as the Local Content Bill) would institute major changes in Nigeria's hydrocarbon sector. The former, which had not yet passed the National Assembly as of this writing, would allocate a larger share of joint venture revenue to the NNPC. The private oil companies have consistently opposed the bill and indicated that it would deter investment and cost Nigeria revenue in the long run. Shell, for instance, has stated that it will forgo $50 billion in planned investment in Nigeria if the bill becomes law (Burgis, 2010). The company representatives indicated to us that the uncertainty surrounding the bill has already slowed investment.

ness they have of events in the vicinity of their installations, the better. Ideally, they would like this to include early warning of an impending assault on an installation, which would give them at least 30 minutes to shut down operations and go into a defensive mode.

The oil companies' representatives emphasized that they had no command and control authority over Nigerian military or police forces. While recognizing shortfalls in the training and equipment of Nigerian-supplied security, the oil companies appear reluctant to directly employ private armed guards or to provide payments or equipment directly to these Nigerian forces. Motivating this reticence are local and international legal and moral considerations. These companies do not want to be associated with any misdeeds the Nigerians might commit against the local population.

One representative observed that, because of the widespread resentment of the federal government in the delta, providing assistance to the military could be seen as "taking sides" and increasing repression. Certain of the oil companies work very hard to maintain an understanding with the armed groups, and after there is an attack, a representative from the company will sometimes try to speak with them to "smooth things over."[2] In 2004, one company formalized understandings with the militants and delta residents through memorandums of understanding and contracts and created regional development councils run by the local population. This has improved the climate and, in return, diminished attacks on that company's facilities.[3]

---

[2]   Interview with oil company representatives, June 25, 2010.

[3]   Interview with oil company representatives, June 25, 2010.

Bibliography

Ahlbrandt, Thomas S., "Oil and Natural Gas Liquids: Global Magnitude and Distribution," *Encyclopedia of Energy*, Vol. 4, Boston: Elsevier Academic Press, 2004.

Akpabio, Emmanuel M., and Nseabasi S. Akpan, "Governance and Oil Politics in Nigeria's Niger Delta: The Question of Distributive Equity," *Journal of Human Ecology*, May 2010.

Arab Press Service, "Nigeria—IOC Partners' Role in Deep-Water Oil & Gas," *APS Review Oil Market Trends*, Vol. 73, No. 6, August 10, 2009.

Areguamen, Oamen, "Nigeria: Enugu Gets Helicopter School," *Vanguard*, January 12, 2010. As of September 15, 2010:
http://www.vanguardngr.com/2010/01/enugu-gets-helicopter-school/

Armstrong Atlantic State University, *Air Assault School*, 2005. As of September 15, 2010:
http://www.rotc.armstrong.edu/TrainingAAS.htm.

Asuni, Judith Burdin, *Blood Oil in the Niger Delta*, United States Institute of Peace Special Report, No. 229, August 2009a.

———, "Understanding the Armed Groups of the Niger Delta," working paper, Washington, D.C.: Council on Foreign Relations, September 2009b.

Barkindo, Mohammed, "Undiscovered Oil Potential Still Large Off West Africa," *Oil & Gas Journal*, January 8, 2007.

Bartis, James T., *Promoting International Energy Security*, Vol. 1: *Understanding Potential Air Force Roles*, Santa Monica, Calif.: RAND Corporation, TR-1144/1-AF, 2012. As of September 4, 2012:
http://www.rand.org/pubs/technical_reports/TR1144z1.html

Bartis, James T., and Lawrence Van Bibber, *Alternative Fuels for Military Applications*, Santa Monica, Calif.: RAND Corporation, MG-969-OSD, 2011. As of June 5, 2011:
http://www.rand.org/pubs/monographs/MG969.html

BBC News, "Nigeria militants 'end truce in Delta oil region,'" January 30, 2010. As of September 15, 2010:
http://news.bbc.co.uk/2/hi/africa/8488772.stm.

———, "Profile: Nigeria's Goodluck Jonathan," April 18, 2011. As of May 17 2011:
http://www.bbc.co.uk/news/world-africa-12192152

Bergen Risk Solutions, *Niger Delta Maritime Security*, Vol. 1, No. 1, July 2007.

BP, *BP Statistical Review of World Energy 2011*, London, June 2011. As of June 30, 2011:
http://www.bp.com/statisticalreview

Briggs, James, "Guide to the Armed Groups Operating in the Niger Delta—Part 2," *Terrorism Monitor*, Vol. 5, No. 8, April 26, 2007.

Burgis, Tom, "New Bill Puts Nigeria's Deepwater Oil Industry on Hold," Beyond Brics blog, June 17, 2010. As of September 15, 2010:
http://blogs.ft.com/beyond-brics/2010/06/17/new-bill-puts-nigerias-deepwater-oil-industry-on-hold/

Charpentier, Ronald R., "Global Distribution of Natural Gas Resources," *Encyclopedia of Energy*, Vol. 4, Boston: Elsevier Academic Press, 2004.

Chevron, *Annual Report 2008*. As of August 30, 2011:
http://www.chevron.com/annualreport/2008/deliveringenergy/deliverenergynow/agbami/

———, *Natural Gas: Providing an Efficient, Economical Energy Source*, March 2010. As of March 22, 2010:
http://www.chevron.com/deliveringenergy/naturalgas/

———, *Nigeria fact sheet*, March 2011. As of March 28, 2011:
http://www.chevron.com/documents/pdf/nigeriafactsheet.pdf

Crane, Keith, Andreas Goldthau, Michael Toman, Thomas Light, Stuart E. Johnson, Alireza Nader, Angel Rabasa, and Harun Dogo, *Imported Oil and National Security*, Santa Monica, Calif.: RAND Corporation, MG-838-USCC, 2009. As of August 30, 2011:
http://www.rand.org/pubs/monographs/MG838.html

Daly, John C. K., "Nigeria's Navy Struggles with Attacks on Offshore Oil Facilities," *Terrorism Monitor*, Vol. 6, No. 14, July 2008.

Davis, Stephen, "Shifting Trends in Oil Theft in the Niger Delta," Legaloil.com Information Paper 3, 2007. As of June 23, 2011:
http://www.legaloil.com/LibraryItem.asp?DocumentIDX=1293653082&Category=library

———, *The Opportunity for Peace in the Niger Delta*, Washington, D.C.: Paul H. Nitze School of Advanced International Studies, Johns Hopkins University, 2009a.

———, *The Potential for Peace and Reconciliation in the Niger Delta*, Coventry, U.K.: Coventry Cathedral, February, 2009b. As of June 23, 2011:
http://www.coventrycathedral.org.uk/downloads/publications/35.pdf

de Zardain, Paul, "New Beginnings," *Gabon Magazine*, London: Impact Media Group Global, Ltd., Summer 2011. As of June 5, 2012:
http://www.gabonmagazine.com/issues.html

DiPaola, Anthony, "Dubai's Oman Crude Futures Is 'The Shot' at New Gulf Benchmark, Vitol Says," Bloomberg News, June 24, 2010. As of October 27, 2010:
http://www.bloomberg.com/news/2010-06-23/dubai-s-oman-crude-futures-is-the-shot-at-new-gulf-benchmark-vitol-says.html

Duffield, Caroline, "Will Amnesty Bring Peace to Niger Delta?" *BBC News*, October 5, 2009. As of May 17, 2011:
http://news.bbc.co.uk/2/mobile/africa/8291336.stm

Edirin, Etaghene, "Nigeria: MEND's Fresh Resurgence As Yar'Adua's Absence Enters 2nd Month," *All Africa*, January 3, 2010. As of May 17, 2011:
http://allafrica.com/stories/201001041239.html

Energy Information Administration, *Country Analysis Briefs: Nigeria*, Washington, D.C.: United States Department of Energy, July 2010. As of June 30, 2011:
http://www.eia.doe.gov/cabs/Nigeria/pdf.pdf

———, *International Energy Statistics*, Washington, D.C.: United States Department of Energy, 2011. As of June 21, 2011:
http://www.eia.gov/countries/data.cfm

Fabiani, Riccardo, "Is the Trans-Sahara Gas Pipeline a Viable Project? The Impact of Terrorism Risk," *Terrorism Monitor*, Vol. 7, No. 25, August 2009.

Giroux, Jennifer, "Turmoil in the Delta: Trends and Implications," *Perspectives on Terrorism*, Vol. 2, No. 8, 2008.

Giroux, Jennifer, and Caroline Hilpert, "The Relationship Between Energy Infrastructure Attacks and Crude Oil Prices," *Journal of Energy Security*, October 2009.

Hartley, Will, and Chanel White, *JTIC Country Briefing—Nigeria*, Jane's Terrorism and Insurgency Centre, February 1, 2009.

Harvest Natural Resources, "Harvest Natural Resources Announces Pre-Salt Ruche Oil Discovery Offshore Gabon," Houston, July 21, 2011. As of November 21, 2011:
http://investor.shareholder.com/harvestnr/releasedetail.cfm?ReleaseID=593200

Hazen, Jennifer M., and Jonas Horner, "Small Arms, Armed Violence and Insecurity in Nigeria: The Niger Delta in Perspective," Occasional Paper No. 20, *Small Arms Survey*, December 2007.

Henry, Ryan, Christine Osowski, Peter Chalk, and James T. Bartis, *Promoting International Energy Security*, Vol. 3: *Sea-Lanes to Asia*, Santa Monica, Calif.: RAND Corporation, TR-1144/3-AF, 2012. As of September 4, 2012:
http://www.rand.org/pubs/technical_reports/TR1144z3.html

Human Rights Watch, *Criminal Politics: Violence, "Godfathers" and Corruption in Nigeria*, New York: 2007. As of June 23, 2011:
http://www.hrw.org/en/reports/2007/10/08/criminal-politics-0

ICC International Maritime Bureau, *Piracy and Armed Robbery Against Ships Annual Report*: 1 January– 31 December 2009, London, U.K., January 2010.

ICG—*See* International Crisis Group.

International Crisis Group, *Fueling the Niger Delta Crisis*, Brussels, Belgium, September 28, 2006. As of September 15, 2010:
http://www.crisisgroup.org/en/regions/africa/west-africa/nigeria/118-fuelling-the-niger-delta-crisis.aspx

———, *Nigeria: Want in the Midst of Plenty*, Brussels, Belgium, July 19, 2006. As of September 15, 2010:
http://www.crisisgroup.org/~/media/Files/africa/west-africa/nigeria/Nigeria%20Want%20in%20the%20 Midst%20of%20Plenty.ashx

———, *Nigeria Seizing the Moment in the Niger Delta*, Brussels, Belgium, April 30, 2009.

International Hydrographic Organization, "Limits of Oceans and Seas," 3rd ed., 1953. As of September 17, 2010:
http://www.iho-ohi.net/iho_pubs/standard/S-23/S23_1953.pdf

International Institute for Strategic Studies, *Military Balance 2011*, London, U.K., 2011.

Jane's Information Group, "Ghana—Air Force," *Jane's World Air Forces*, November 30, 2009.

———, "Nigeria—Navy," *Jane's World Navies*, July 8, 2010a.

———, "Nigeria—Air Force," *Jane's World Air Forces*, November 7, 2010b.

———, "Nigeria," *Jane's Sentinel Security Assessment West Africa*, April 19, 2011.

———, "Air Force, Nigeria," *Jane's Sentinel Security Assessment West Africa*, March 19, 2012.

———, Jane's Terrorism Insurgency Centre, *JTIC Country Briefing: Nigeria*, 2009.

Junger, Sebastian, "Blood Oil," *Vanity Fair*, February 2007.

Kasmierski, Daniel, U.S. Africa Command, correspondence, May 21, 2010.

Kaufmann, Daniel, Aart Kraay, and Massimo Mastruzzi, "The Worldwide Governance Indicators: Methodology and Analytical Issues," World Bank Policy Research Working Paper No. 5430, Washington, D.C.: The World Bank, September 2010. As of November 17, 2010:
http://ssrn.com/abstract=1682130

Kington, Tom, "Nigeria Becomes 1st Export Customer for ATR 42MP," Defense News, December 10, 2009.

Lewis, Peter M., *Nigeria: Assessing Risks to Stability*, Washington, D.C.: Center for Strategic and International Studies, 2011.

Lloyd, Alec, "U.S. Air Forces Africa Help Nigerian C-130 Fly Again," U.S. Africa Command, September 1, 2009. As of September 15, 2010:
http://www.africom.mil/getArticle.asp?art=3381

Mazumdar, Mrityunjoy, "Chasing the Dream: Nigerian Navy Plays Catch-Up as President Seeks Top 20 Spot," *Jane's Navy International*, September 24, 2009.

Mbiriri, Rutendo, "Nigeria's Deep Water Oil Fields: Cause for Contestation," *Consultancy Africa Intelligence,* November 1, 2009. As of February 27, 2010:
http://www.consultancyafrica.com/index.php?option=com_content&view=article&id=284&Itemid=190

Moroney, Jennifer D. P., Joe Hogler, Jefferson P. Marquis, Christopher Paul, John E. Peters, and Beth Grill, *Developing an Assessment Framework for U.S. Air Force Building Partnerships Programs,* Santa Monica, Calif.: RAND Corporation, MG-868-AF, 2010. As of August 30, 2011:
http://www.rand.org/pubs/monographs/MG868.html

"Nigeria Attack Stops Shells Bonga Offshore Oil," Reuters, June 19, 2008.

"Nigeria: Cults of Violence," *The Economist,* Vol. 388, No. 8591, July 31, 2008.

"Nigerian Attack Closes Oilfield," BBC News, June 20, 2008.

Nigerian National Petroleum Corporation, *2009 Annual Statistical Bulletin,* Abuja, Nigeria, 2010. As of March 31, 2012:
http://www.nnpcgroup.com/PublicRelations/OilandGasStatistics/AnnualStatisticsBulletin.aspx

———, *Exploration and Production, 2010.* As of February 27, 2010:
http://http://www.nnpcgroup.com/directorates/exploration-a-production

Nossiter, Adam, "Far from Gulf, a Spill Scourge 5 Decades Old," *New York Times,* June 16, 2010.

Obasi, Nnamdi, "Nigeria: Yar'Adua Should Draw Up Roadmap to Delta Peace," AllAfrica.com, November 30, 2009.

Petrobras, "Acquisition of Exploration Blocks in Gabon," Form 6-K filing with the U.S. Securities and Exchange Commission, File number 1-15106, Rio de Janeiro, June 17, 2011.

Sandrea, Rafael, and Ivan Sandrea, "Deepwater Crude Output: How Large Will the Uptick Be?" *Oil and Gas Journal,* November 1, 2010.

Shell Nigeria, "Shell at a Glance—Nigeria," 2010. As of February 27, 2010:
http://www.shell.com.ng/home/content/nga/aboutshell/at_a_glance/

Sirleaf, Ellen Johnson, "The 100 Most Influential People in the World: Goodluck Jonathan," April 18, 2012. As of May 17, 2011:
http://www.time.com/time/specials/packages/article/0,28804,2111975_2111976_2112110,00.html

Tattersall, Nick, "Nigeria Attack Stops Shell's Bonga Offshore Oil," Reuters, June 19, 2008.

The World Bank, *Nigeria: Country Brief,* April 2010. As of September 17, 2010:
http://go.worldbank.org/FIIOT240K0

Tullow Oil Ghana, Overview—Jubilee field—Key facts, web page, July 6, 2010. As of September 15, 2010:
http://www.tullowoil.com/ghana/index.asp?pageid=30

———, "Interim Management Statement," press release dated November 9, 2011. As of November 25, 2011:
http://www.tullowoil.com/GHANA/index.asp?pageid=43&newsid=715

Tuttle, Michele L. W., Ronald R. Charpentier, and Michael E. Brownfield, *The Niger Delta Petroleum System: Niger Delta Province, Nigeria,* Cameroon, and Equatorial Guinea, Africa, Open-File Report 99-50-H, Washington, D.C.: U.S. Geological Survey, U.S. Department of the Interior, 1999. As of February 27, 2010:
http://pubs.usgs.gov/of/1999/ofr-99-0050/OF99-50H/

U.S. Air Force, *Air Force Basic Doctrine,* USAF Doctrine Document 1, November 17, 2003. As of September 15, 2010:
http://www.dtic.mil/doctrine/jel/service_pubs/afdd1.pdf

U.S. Coast Guard, *SAR Program Information,* U.S. Department of Homeland Security, April 2009. As of September 15, 2010:
http://www.uscg.mil/hq/cg5/cg534/SAR_Program_Info.asp

U.S. Department of Defense, *Quadrennial Defense Review Report,* Washington, D.C., February 2010.

U.S. Department of State, "2009 Human Rights Report: Nigeria," Bureau of Democracy, Human Rights, and Labor, March 11, 2010a. As of June 5, 2012:
http://www.state.gov/j/drl/rls/hrrpt/2009/af/135970.htm

———, "2010 Human Rights Report: Equatorial Guinea," Bureau of Democracy, Human Rights, and Labor, April 2011b. As of November 22, 2011:
http://www.state.gov/g/drl/rls/hrrpt/

———, "Background Note: Equatorial Guinea," Bureau of African Affairs, October 28, 2011c. As of November 22, 2011:
http://www.state.gov/r/pa/ei/bgn/7221.htm

U.S. Department of the Navy, *Navy Search and Rescue Tactical Information Document* (SAR TACAID), NWP 3-22.5-SAR-TAC, Office of the Chief of Naval Operations, September 1997.

U.S. Geological Survey, *USGS World Petroleum Assessment 2000*, USGS FS–062–03, Washington, D.C.: U.S. Department of the Interior, June 2003.

Ukpohor, Excel Theophilus O., "Nigerian Gas Master Plan: Strengthening the Nigeria Gas Infrastructure Blueprint as a Base for Expanding Regional Gas Market," World Gas Conference technical paper, 2009. As of March 22, 2010:
http://www.igu.org/html/wgc2009/papers/docs/wgcFinal00764.pdf

Vogelaar, Rob, "Alenia Aeronautica Delivers Second ATR-42MP Airplane to the NAF," *Aviation News*, March 29, 2010. As of September 15, 2010:
http://www.avionews.com/index.php?corpo=see_news_home.php&news_id=1115873&pagina_chiamante=index.php

Walker, Andrew, "Nigeria's Gas Profits 'Up in Smoke,'" BBC News, January 13, 2009. As of March 22, 2010:
http://news.bbc.co.uk/2/hi/africa/7820384.stm

Watkins, Eric, "Nigerian Militants Threaten Proposed Trans-Sahara Gas Line," *Oil and Gas Journal*, July 12, 2009.

Weiss, Andrew S., F. Stephen Larrabee, James T. Bartis, and Camille Sawak, *Promoting International Energy Security*, Vol. 2: *Turkey and the Caspian*, Santa Monica: Calif.: RAND Corporation, TR-1144/2-AF, 2012. As of September 4, 2012:
http://www.rand.org/pubs/technical_reports/TR1144z2.html

Wellington, Bestman, "Nigeria's Cults and Their Role in the Niger Delta Insurgency," *Terrorism Monitor*, Vol. 5, No. 13, July 6, 2007.

The White House, *National Security Strategy*, Washington, D.C., May 2010.

Yergin, Daniel, Chairman of Cambridge Energy Research Associates, "Oil at the Break Point," testimony before the U.S. Congress Joint Economic Committee in Washington, D.C., June 25, 2008. As of February 27, 2010:
http://www2.cera.com/news/DYergin_June2008_Testimony.pdf

Yoon, Mi Yung, "European Colonialism and Territorial Disputes in Africa: The Gulf of Guinea and the Indian Ocean," *Mediterranean Quarterly*, Vol. 20, No. 2, Spring 2009, pp. 77–94.

Zaney, Gordon Deku, "Petroleum Security Coordinating Committee Inaugurated," Information Services Department, Ghana Ministry of Information, January 19, 2011. As of November 25, 2011:
http://ghana.gov.gh/index.php/news/general-news/4542-petroleum-security-coordinating-committee-inaugurated